Masters of
IMPRESSIONISM

Masters of
IMPRESSIONISM

Trewin Copplestone

Published in 1998 by
Regency House Publishing Limited
3 Mill Lane, Broxbourne
Herts EN10 7AZ
England

Printed in Italy

ISBN 0-7666-0291-5
UPC 00243

Contents

Pierre-Auguste Renoir

Trewin Copplestone

List of Plates

PLATE 1
Photograph of Pierre-Auguste Renoir

The history of Impressionism includes a few painters who are central to its development and a large number who are peripheral but nonetheless important because they add some small piece to the large jigsaw that is the Impressionist revolution. There are perhaps four painters at the centre of the movement, each contributing something essential in its initial creative stages. The four are Monet, Pissarro, Sisley and Renoir, the role and contribution offered by Renoir being the least easy to define. His participation in the creation of what has become known as Impressionism is unquestionable and during the period that he was working closely with him, his work certainly has an affinity with Monet's. But outside this relatively short association of a little more than a decade, Renoir's work goes through a number of developments, both before and after, that appear to have but little connection with the characteristics that are familiarly Impressionist. However, the general character and philosophy of the movement will be recognized in his work. Perhaps what it is important to establish is the earlier development of Renoir's life before he encountered those painters in whose company the stylistic and philosophical character was developed, and also to examine the work that he produced after the break-up of the movement into independent directions after the last Impressionist exhibition in 1886.

One general point, however, is undoubtedly true;

Renoir has been for so long and so positively described as an Impressionist that, however difficult it may be to accommodate his work at some stages, he will always be known as an Impressionist. This may be unfair to his overall aims and achievement and limit recognition of his non-Impressionist work, even to devalue it. Further, his artistic aims, his attitude to painting as declared by him and revealed in his temperament are ultimately far from that of other Impressionists, Monet or Pissarro for instance, however superficially similar they may seem. Of course, this is not surprising; as we are constantly being reminded, we are all different with a unique experience and philosophy. Nor do we remain through life the same individual as when we began it. Renoir, at the age of 22 when in the studio of Gleyre, learning methods and technique as a student with Monet and Bazille, had been accused by Gleyre on one occasion of 'seeming to take painting as a pleasure', Renoir's reply: 'Quite true, if painting were not a pleasure to me I certainly should not do it.' This is perhaps a more significant remark than even Renoir knew since from the beginning of his working life he was in search not only of satisfaction in labour, a job well done, but pleasure, and even delight, in what he did.

His life did not start propitiously. Pierre-Auguste Renoir was born at Limoges, in central France, on 25 February 1841 the fourth of five children. Two painters, both part of the Impressionist revolution, and later to

PLATE 2
The Painter Lacoeur in the Forest of Fontainebleau (1866)
Oil on canvas, 41³/₄ x 31¹/₂ inches (106 x 80cm)

The influence of two of Renoir's early mentors can be seen in this painting. The general effect of the work shows the quality of Courbet in its heavy paint and sturdy drawing and in its plein-air treatment in the Forest of Fontainebleau, the impact of Diaz's admonition to him two years earlier to stop using black. Painted while he was staying at Marlotte, near Fontainebleau, the painting represents only one aspect of Renoir's style at that time since, while at Marlotte, he also painted The Inn of Mother Anthony, *a scene at the inn at which he stayed, with his friends, Monet, Bazille and Sisley all depicted in it. This painting is dark and with much black and linear outlining.*

PLATE 3
Portrait of Frédéric Bazille (1867)
Oil on canvas, 41¹/₃ x 29 inches (105 x 73.5cm)

Bazille, born in Montpellier, had originally been expected by his father to follow a medical career but the attraction of painting drew him to Paris and Gleyre's atelier where he met Monet, Sisley and Renoir and they were close friends until Bazille was killed in the Franco-Prussian War of 1870. Bazille was talented, and painted his friends in their studios as well as himself acting as a model for them. He was tall and thin, as is evident in the crouching pose in this painting, and he is consequently easily recognizable in their paintings. For example, he appears twice in Monet's Déjeuner sur l'herbe. *Renoir's style at this time still owes much to Courbet and is not an 'Impressionist' work. It is constructed on the academic tonal method and is far closer to Manet than the paintings of his friends.*

become his friends, Frédéric Bazille and Berthe Morisot, were born in the same year. Renoir's father was a small-time tailor who despite making a meagre living appears to have been concerned for his sons' futures as well as wishing to improve his own circumstances, and moved with his family to Paris when Pierre was 4. Although he had little means, he nevertheless was interested in *objets d'art* in a way that many of the *petite bourgeoisie* were, and even hoped that his sons might have work of an artistic, if humble, kind. Renoir's mother, too, had a sensitive nature and was accustomed to taking her sons for walks in the woods, drawing their attention to the beauty and endless variety of nature.

Pierre-Auguste was a good-humoured and serious-minded youth with a conscientious spirit. At school in Paris he showed an early talent for drawing and had a good ear for music. He sang in the choir of the local church where the then unknown Gounod was choirmaster. One of his brothers had already shown an inclination towards the arts and was an heraldic engraver when, at the age of 13, Pierre-Auguste was apprenticed to a china manufacturer, a trade that was part of the proud traditional heritage of Limoges. His father hoped that he would have a profession for life as a painter on porcelain and might even become a painter in the great porcelain factory at Sèvres, then on the outskirts of Paris.

Renoir was later to recall that it was his job to

PLATE 4
Lise with a Parasol (1867) opposite
Oil on canvas, 71²/₃ x 46¹/₂ inches (182 x 118cm)

PLATE 5
Boy with a Cat (1868) below
Oil on canvas, 48¹/₂ x 26 inches (123 x 66cm)

At this time, Renoir was hoping to make an income from portrait-painting and submitted to the Salon each year after his Esmeralda Dancing with her Goat was accepted in 1863, other works being rejected in 1864, accepted in 1865, and refused in 1865, 1866 and 1867. His Lise with a Parasol was accepted in 1868. Lise Tréhot was 16 when Renoir painted her, and he saw her as an ideal subject, physically mature but still retaining the freshness of youth. The portrait shows the influence of Manet in the dramatic opposition of dark navy-blue belt and sash and brilliant white dress, but with its closely modelled paint treatment and careful drawing of an atmospheric sun-dappled background not derived from Manet.

This strange and unusual study was undertaken when Renoir was concerned with the academic qualities of draughtsmanship and he made a number of nude studies which usually acquired a classical title. A painting of a nude Lise from the previous year was turned into a 'Diana' by the addition of a dead deer and an archer's bow. In this painting no such alternative seems obvious and the careful drawing of the figure and the fat contented cat remain an example of Renoir's pursuit at this time of fine painting within the academic tradition.

'sprinkle tiny bouquets on a white ground, for which I was paid five sous a dozen', adding that the unscrupulous manufacturer stamped everything with the Sèvres trademark. Renoir progressed in his work to such an extent that he eventually received eight sous for profiles of Marie Antoinette! Unfortunately, as it seemed at the time, the factory was forced to close in 1858 when the development of machine decoration made hand-painted porcelain too expensive to produce. However, Renoir had learned much that was to be of value to him later. He had learned to paint delicately with thin pointed brushes and to use paint to create a striking luminosity.

While at the factory he had also developed an interest in art and in his lunch break visited the Louvre, being especially fascinated by Goujon's *Fontaine des Innocents*, 1547-49. His interest in sculptural form was aroused by this work and by the visits he made in the evenings to the studio of a sculptor who was also employed in his factory. He was particularly attracted by the full and rounded female forms of the models in his friend's studio and they became a recurrent feature of his later work.

When the factory closed Renoir had to look for work of a different kind. For a time he painted decorative fans – 'God knows how many times I copied the *Embarkation for Cythera*!' He claimed that the first painters he got to know were Watteau, Lancret and Boucher, the great rococo artists of the early 18th century in France. Boucher's *Bath*

PLATE 6
Bather with her Griffon (1870)
Oil on canvas, 72½ x 45¼ inches (184 x 115cm)

The subject of this painting is again Lise Tréhot but without the classical trappings. In this painting Renoir was influenced by the work of Courbet and the pose is reminiscent of him. The fact that the dog is a griffon, a creature with mythological

associations, may have some significance since he submitted it to the Salon of 1870 and it was accepted. While he was exploring pictorial possibilities with such paintings as those he produced while working with Monet at La Grenouillère, Renoir continued to paint more traditional subjects, particularly nude studies for exhibition at the Salon, remarking that if showing at the Salon did no good, it at least did no harm.

of Diana, a voluptuously exotic nude, remained a favourite painting – perhaps reinforcing his interest in the female form. The fan-painting provided him with only a pittance and he abandoned it when offered the somewhat curious opportunity of painting blinds for missionaries. These were intended to take the place of stained-glass windows in their far-flung improvised places of worship. Thus, from the exotic subjects of the fans he turned to religious subjects, the most popular apparently being the 'Adoration of the Magi' and 'St. Vincent de Paul'. He produced these with such speed and facility that he was soon making and saving money. His personal ambition, the drudgery of the repetitious work and the fact the he had some money, encouraged him to pursue a life of art. He had survived life as an artisan with limited horizons with his cheerful spirit intact and he looked forward to learning the higher levels of painting with keen anticipation.

In 1862, at the age of 21, Renoir took courses at the École des Beaux Arts and at the same time entered the studio of Gabriel-Charles Gleyre, mentioned earlier, a Swiss painter who had come to Paris and taken over the former studio of a successful academic painter, Paul Delaroche. He, too, was a successful teacher and his atelier was one of the most popular in Paris. Once there, he met as fellow students Monet, Sisley and Bazille. Whistler had also been a student with Gleyre but had left before Renoir arrived. Renoir was not impressed or inspired by Gleyre's teaching and with

others left the following year, galvanized by a visit to a show by Manet at Martinet's gallery and, finally, by the Salon des Refusés, a seminal occasion for the development of Impressionism.

The importance for these young students of the Salon des Refusés cannot be over-emphasized. Édouard Manet, a painter only a little older than Renoir, in 1863 submitted to the annual Salon held in the Grand Salon of the Louvre (hence the name) to which all the great academicians sent their latest work and in which Renoir actually had a painting accepted, *Esmeralda Dancing with her Goat*. The Salon was the most important Parisian artistic gathering of the year and was that year opened by the emperor Napoleon III. In the course of general conversation, Napoleon suggested that the rejected paintings should be shown in other vacant rooms in the palace, thus emphasizing by comparison the superiority of the main Salon, and suggested that the exhibition be called the Salon des Refusés. Naturally, he was taken seriously. Manet's painting was one of those not accepted for the Salon and thus found its way into the Salon des Refusés. Called *Le déjeuner sur l'herbe*, it caused such a serious scandal that the Refusés experiment was not repeated. This, however, had the effect of making the notorious Manet even more attractive to the young independently minded young painters at the time, including the four at Gleyre's.

Manet's painting was of an unusual picnic scene

Continued on page 21

PLATE 7
La Grenouillère (c. 1869)
Oil on canvas, 23¹/₄ x 31¹/₂ inches (59 x 80cm)

Although painted round about the same time as the previous work, Renoir here reveals an evident progress towards Impressionism. And this is perhaps not surprising when it is recalled that he painted with Monet at this time and La Grenouillère was a favourite recreation spot for Parisians. La Grenouillère was on Croissy Island in the Seine near Bougival and was, in a contemporary report, ' ...inhabited by a swarm of writers, men and women belonging to the artistic life of Paris ... along the banks at certain hours of the day, sometimes fishing, sometimes for the pleasure of bathing in open water.' It became a social fad when Louis Napoléon and Eugénie condescended to visit the place in 1869. Monet and Renoir, neither of them permanently located, naturally gravitated here and painted side-by-side, each to some degree influencing the other. It was a preparatory stage in the evolution that took definite form at Argenteuil in the early 1870s.

PLATE 8
Portrait of Claude Monet (1872)
Oil on canvas, 24 x 19²/₃ inches (61 x 50cm)

At this time, Renoir had a studio in Paris and stayed and painted with Monet at Argenteuil. They had a close and friendly working *relationship and Renoir participated in the first Impressionist exhibition arranged by Monet and Degas. This is not a characteristic Impressionist work although the short brushstrokes owe something to Monet, the density of the dark near-black over large areas of the canvas giving solidity to form rather than light.*

PLATE 9
Portrait of Claude Monet (1875)
Oil on canvas, 33½ x 23¾ inches (85 x 60.5cm)

Comparison with the portrait painted three years earlier (plate 8) reveals how far Renoir had travelled towards an Impressionist technique of small touches – sometimes described as 'comma' strokes – with undefined outlines and a pervading sense of light. The painting was exhibited in the second Impressionist exhibition and was well received by the critics. Renoir made a number of portraits of Monet around this time, including one of Monet painting in his garden at Argenteuil. Although this and the previous painting may be taken to be part of Impressionism, Renoir was always searching for new means of expression and his style during the period of the 1870s varies so much that Renoir's Impressionism, unlike Monet's, has no clear indisputable identity.

Continued from page 16

containing two elegantly dressed young men-about-town reclining on the grass accompanied by a naked female who is looking directly out of the picture at the viewer, bold-eyed and challenging. The fourth figure in the background is a scantily-clad female in the act of either robing or disrobing. It will be appreciated that nudes were familiar subjects for paintings, but were usually of such personages as Venus, Aphrodite, Hercules or Mercury which introduced an aura of unreality, antiquity and a link with the past history of art, being idealized and remote rather than merely plain naked. Not a wisp of body hair was visible and most such compositions were, in addition, given titles with classical and mythological associations such as the 'Garden of the Hesperides', and portrayed figures engaged in obscure pageants. As it happens, Manet had intended to modernize, to actualize in the present a composition taken from a painting by Raphael and probably seen by Manet in the form of an engraving by Marcantonio Raimondi. Manet, with this single painting, had fatally wounded the intellectual pretensions of the Académie and had demonstrated the possibilities of everyday life as a subject for the modern painter.

It took just over a decade for the impact of this painting, together with another of Manet's exhibited in 1865 and this time accepted by the Salon, called *Olympia*, another nude but reclining on a bed and again confronting

the viewer with the kind of bold invitation of women displaying themselves in lighted windows in Amsterdam. Another *succès de scandale*, it reinforced Manet's somewhat reluctant role as leader of the avant garde of young painters who began to meet in Manet's favourite Café Guerbois in the avenue de Clichy in the Batignolles district of Paris. These included Monet, Degas, Bazille and Renoir who, despite the urgent discussion which was a feature of their meetings, hardly spoke. He was not a theorist.

After leaving Gleyre's atelier, Renoir shared a studio with Bazille where the group also met. Each had their own personal enthusiasms for particular artists from outside the dimensions of the academic world. For Renoir, it was Diaz de la Peña, a member of the so-called Barbizon school who painted in the open-air in and around the Forest of Fontainebleau and included Millet, Rousseau, Dubigny, Dupré, Troyon and Diaz, all of whom influenced one or more of the Impressionists with their devotion to the landscape in which they lived and worked. At the first meeting between Diaz and Renoir in the forest where he was working, Diaz's advice to Renoir was that he should stop using black, a suggestion he immediately accepted with the result that he destroyed the painting that he had exhibited in the Salon of 1863. It was a turning-point in his career and the subsequent influence of Courbet and Manet must be added to the influences which affected a sea-change in Renoir's painting.

PLATE 10
La Loge (Box at the Theatre) 1874
Oil on canvas, 31½ x 24¾ inches (80 x 63cm)

For the affluent middle classes, Parisian life usually involved the regular attendance at theatrical entertainments where people went to see and be seen, which was possibly more important to them than the performance. This elegant and famous painting, one of Renoir's most delicate evocations of French society, reflects his delight in attractive women in privileged circumstances. Or so it seems: but in fact he chose a well known Montmartre model dressed in a startling broad-striped gown to portray a well-heeled society lady and his brother Edmond as the man-about-town in the background. Renoir's patrons for his main source of commissioned portraits would have been impressed by this pictorial tour de force, executed in thin paint and a strong tonal range. The significance of the location is also important and was a popular subject for illustration and portraiture. The theatre box would have been a natural location for the privileged, like Manet or Degas, but for Renoir, with his bourgeois background, it was an effort to enter into such a milieu which would provide him with the sitters he needed. The emphatic presentation of the figures in close-up (the man is hardly given sufficient depth in space to occupy) adds one more element of exciting immediacy, and the angle of the edge of the box on which the woman's hand rests is indicated in such a way as to suggest that the viewer is also in the next box – a participant in the event. Although this is a traditional treatment and Renoir uses black – a non-Impressionist colour but which Renoir described as the 'queen of colours' – he exhibited this work in the first Impressionist exhibition and it has become one of the most admired masterpieces of the Impressionist movement.

In the years approaching 1870 and the outbreak of the Franco-Prussian War, Renoir continued to submit work to the Salon which was sometimes accepted, sometimes not. He experimented in an almost carefree manner with various techniques, on occasion using the heavy impasto of Courbet, sometimes the strong contrasts in brushstrokes of Manet. He was also beginning to associate closely with the proto-Impressionists. In 1869, for instance, he went to Louveciennes to see Pissarro as well as his own parents who also lived there.

The Franco-Russian War had a dramatic effect on the lives of the painters. Degas and Manet served in the French army, Monet and Pissarro avoided conscription by escaping to England, as did Sisley who was English although born in Paris. Bazille also joined the army but was unfortunately killed. Cézanne, disregarding call-up papers, went south to L'Estaque. Renoir, with his *laisser-faire* attitude, allowed matters to take their course, ended up in the army and was posted to Bordeaux, far from military action. When the war ended he remained in the area, painting happily for a time. His comment on his army career: 'I could nail down ammunition boxes like no one else – my captain found that I was possessed of the military spirit and wanted me to continue my life in the army.' In his characteristically light-hearted way he observed that had he taken up all the careers people had encouraged him to follow, what a life he would have had.

Once freed from the army and after two or three months, Renoir returned to Paris in search of portrait commissions and to paint the life of the city which was dear to his heart. He began to renew his friendships with his former associates. Particularly important at this time was the role taken by Monet who had replaced Manet as leader, much to that gentleman's relief. After the war, Monet had moved to Argenteuil, a small town on the outskirts of Paris on the banks of the Seine which became the focus of the group of young independent painters who had gathered around Manet at the Café Guerbois. The Argenteuil association resulted in the group's decision to hold an exhibition since they did not believe they were making enough headway towards the public recognition to which, by then, they considered they were entitled. As already noted, Renoir was not very interested in the various theories, the subjects of many discussions, and he continued to work with the influence of his early inspiration, particularly Courbet and Manet, and this mostly in the matter of technique rather than subject-matter. At this time, the group was not a close-knit organization but a number of independent artists who had similar career aims – to be successful and recognized. It was thus possible for Renoir to be part of the group without subscribing to any specific artistic philosophy.

Another to influence Renoir's technique rather than his subject-matter was Delacroix, whose method of

PLATE 11
Path Winding Upwards through Tall Grass
(c. 1874)
Oil on canvas, 23²/₃ x 29 inches (60 x 74cm)

Renoir varies his technique in response to the exigencies of his subject and his technical assurance by this time enables him to mix his methods to achieve precisely the effect he wishes. The grass in the foreground is painted in thick strokes, sometimes called his comma effect, to create the density he requires, while the background is laid in with thin, flat areas of colour which merge into one another to give the undefined identity of distance. The two figures give a central focus to the picture and are reminiscent of Monet's use of figures in his poppy-field paintings.

applying paint, evidenced by Renoir's painting of 1872, *Parisian Women Dressed as Algerians* (plate 16), was directly inspired by Delacroix's *Women of Algiers*, a painting that has influenced a number of later artists who regarded it as inspirational subject-matter: for instance, Pablo Picasso in the 1950s. The strong painterly qualities of brush and colour which Delacroix produced, with a luscious exoticism, was a far cry from the dry tonal work of the academics, and was not only an important influence on all Impressionists but in Renoir's case returned him to the colour of the Venetians, Titian and Veronese, and to Rubens. For Renoir, Delacroix remained a hero and his *Women of Algiers* was one of Renoir's favourite paintings.

During the 1870s, Renoir was beginning to have some success, was submitting paintings to the Salon – frowned upon by the group, most of whom had abandoned the Salon. Renoir's response was typical: 'My submitting to the Salon is a purely business matter. Like certain medicines: if it doesn't do any good it doesn't do any harm.' During the period he painted some of his best known works including *La Loge*, 1874 (plate 10), *Le Moulin de la Galette,* 1876 (plate 15), *The Swing,* 1876 (plate 17), and *Madame Charpentier and her Children*, 1878 (plate 20).

The result of the discussions, and the fact that members of the group were painting together at Argenteuil, was that the first group exhibition was held in

PLATE 12
Woman Reading (1874–76)
Oil on canvas, 18$\frac{1}{3}$ x 15$\frac{1}{8}$ inches (46.5 x 38.5cm)

Painted around the time of the first Impressionist exhibition, this study is more an examination of a lighting effect than a portrait. Renoir was always alert to different possibilities of subject and technique in combination, and his model with top illumination and reflection from the pages of her book must have posed an attractive problem which he tackled with an Impressionist brush.

PLATE 13
Young Woman Wearing a Veil (1875)
Oil on canvas, 24 x 20 inches (61 x 51cm)

One Impressionist device in portraiture was to create a casual informality of treatment and to achieve this the painters frequently chose to suggest that the sitter was unaware they were being painted and even had them not looking towards the viewer. To this extent the painting is even more typical than the obviously posed figure in the painting opposite. The addition of a veil adds mystery and provides an opportunity for a dramatic opposition between the tartan geometrical check and the small dots of the veil.

PLATE 14
Nude Study: The Effect of Sunlight
(1875–76)
Oil on canvas, 31⅞ x 25½ inches (81 x 65cm)

Although described as a study, this delightful work searches for an effect that is apparent in a number of Renoir's paintings of the period, including the well known Swing *(plate 17), and* Le Moulin de la Galette *(plate 15) – the dappled effect of sunlight through foliage. In Renoir's terms, this is essentially an Impressionist painting, both in intention and treatment. The casual immediacy of the fall of light, changing on the instant, touching a small form in a passing caress, produces a strong sense of the actual visual sensation of a moment in time. The delicate brushstrokes that build the soft fleshly forms are opposed by the roughly indicated background foliage and by the sharp gold-hued bracelet and finger ring the woman wears – an acute reminder of nearby civilization ready to impinge on the idyllic scene.*

1874 at the former studio of the great early photographer, Nadar, and was called the Première Exposition de la Société Anonyme des Artistes, Peintres, Sculpteurs, Graveurs. It opened on 15 April and lasted for one month. It is now more usually known as the first Impressionist exhibition. The name Impressionist was given by a critic, Louis Le Roy, who called his highly antagonistic and sarcastic review of the show the 'Exhibition of the Impressionists' because Monet had entitled one of his paintings *Impression: Sunrise*. The name stuck and this is perhaps unfortunate since it bore little relationship to most of the work in the show, including most of Monet's. Degas, one of the organizers, preferred the appellation Independent or Realist and refused to use the word Impressionist to describe his work. In fact, the work and aims of the group were individually so different that the word Impressionist really in itself carries little meaning. Even in the case of Monet, it is only explicitly applicable for a period in the 1870s and 1880s. As far as Renoir's painting is concerned, his work is certainly close to Monet's during the Argenteuil period but, as has already been noted, Renoir was not a theorist and pursued whatever influences affected him strongly at the time, and these were numerous and with more to come.

Renoir sent seven works to this first show, including one of his much admired paintings, *La Loge* (plate 10). In this same year Renoir met Caillebotte, an amateur painter associated with the Impressionists but, more importantly for them perhaps, a sensitive collector who bought Impressionist works which later included a number of Renoir's. In the following year he met another collector, Victor Chocquet, an amateur painter and customs officer who had little money but a passion for painting, and who collected the works of Delacroix. The meeting occurred through a disastrous auction sale at the Hôtel Drouot of the works of the penurious Impressionists. The sale reflected the ridicule to which the first Impressionist exhibition had been subjected, resulting in such low prices as to seem, by today's standards, incredible. One of Renoir's paintings, *Le Pont Neuf* (1872), fetched a mere 300 francs. In another sale as early as 1910, the same work fetched almost 100,000 francs. Chocquet dropped in at the sale by chance, bought some paintings and became a friend and loyal patron of the group. Chocquet also commissioned Renoir and others in the group to paint portraits of both himself and his wife.

Renoir's Impressionism is generally held to be confined to the period from the time he was in Argenteuil, in about 1872, to the early 1880s. This is not to suggest that all works within that decade carry a specifically Impressionist character – Renoir was far too interested in exploring different methods for this to be true – but his work, together with Monet's, Pissarro's and Sisley's during the period undoubtedly have close affinities. This is

PLATE 15

Le Moulin de la Galette, Montmartre
(1875-76)

Oil on canvas, 51¹/₂ x 68⁷/₈ inches (131 x 175cm)

The Moulin de la Galette was one of the most popular places of entertainment in Montmartre, still then a straggling village on the outskirts of Paris and visited by the Impressionists and their friends and followers for much of the later 19th century. The Montmartre area contained a number of windmills which had fallen into disuse and had either been, like the Galette, turned into taverns, or demolished. The name derived from the speciality of the former mill, a flat biscuit-like cake known as a galette. The property was turned, first into a guinguette, a small restaurant with dancing, and subsequently grew into an open-air dance-hall and café-bar where young people of the locality, rather than high society, thronged on Sundays from 3 p.m. until midnight, in carefree pursuit of pleasure. Entertainments were provided, prostitutes danced happily when not involved in seeking clients (although even Edward, the Prince of Wales, later found a lover there), and seamstresses, laundresses, flower-girls and milliners provided Renoir and his friends with both dancing partners and models.

In Renoir's painting, an interesting combination of dappled sunlight and artificial illumination combine to produce a dancing confusion into which he has placed a number of his friends and their dancing partners, many identifiable through an extensive account by Georges Rivière. Jeanne, seen in The Swing *(plate 17), is in the centre foreground with her arm over her younger sister Estelle. Since Jeanne was only 16 they clearly began to socialize at an early age. It should not be supposed that they were mostly prostitutes, they were hard-working girls, dreaming of making good marriages.*

This is a highly considered and constructed composition, larger than most (nearly 6ft wide) and peopled with many figures. It gives an extraordinarily convincing impression of genuine enjoyment in a large gathering.

PLATE 16

Parisian Women Dressed as Algerians

Oil on canvas, 61³/₄ x 51¹/₂ inches (157 x 131cm)

Since the establishment of Algeria as an exotic and romantic pictorial subject after Renoir's visit there in 1833, many artists had looked to Africa and the Near East for their subject-matter and saw in his work a direct challenge to academic historicism. As a result, not only were his works and his technique copied and adopted by others, but they inspired an atmosphere of pictorial freedom which was attractive to the young independent painters who were to form the Impressionist group. Among these was

Renoir, always alert to possibilities of change and new directions, and he not only made copies of Delacroix's Women of Algiers *but adapted the theme to something which interested him, the female form, which resulted in such curious works as the treatment opposite. The figures here are clearly Renoir's models and Parisian women in a state of undress which is a far cry from Delacroix's example. (Bared breasts and thighs are not a feature of Algerian harem life.) The two models he used are probably Fanny Roberts and Lise Tréhot already seen in plates 4 and 6. The work was painted for the salon of 1872 but was rejected which rather dampened Renoir's ardour for such foreign exoticism.*

certainly not surprising in the early Argenteuil years since the artists often painted the same subject together, views of the same skiff or the bridge at Argenteuil, for example. Renoir and Monet, for instance, painted the same view of the boating scene at La Grenouillère (plate 7), a popular venue on the Seine on the outskirts of Paris. This was also true of other locations; both Renoir and Cézanne painted Mont Sainte-Victoire together and the famous *pigeonnier* at Bellevue, Cézanne's sister's farm, with less than similar results (See plate 35).

It is indeed the diversity of the work of that small group, associated through the 1870s and 1880s and remaining friends though not always in sympathy or having appreciation for each other's work, that engages our interest. So much so, that to extend Impressionism to the last stages of the work of all of them, although perhaps with less truth in the case of Monet, is to look for an identity, a unity that did not exist and to make any such inclusivity of definition in respect of Impressionism a conjunction devoutly to be avoided. As an example: a Cézanne and a Van Gogh of 1889 can only be compared in their differences. By that year each had achieved an individual style that reflected their widely differing philosophies.

In Renoir's case, the Impressionist period lasted from about 1872, just before the first Impressionist exhibition, until 1883, when there was a dramatic change in his

technique. His life from 1872 to 1876 was difficult and, as noted, he submitted with varying success to the Salon; but he was at least helped by the support of Durand-Ruel, one of the two or three important dealers in Impressionist work who continued to purchase paintings from Renoir until Durand-Ruel himself found himself in reduced circumstances due to the failure of his bank.

During this period Renoir hoped to support himself by portraiture and in 1876 met Georges Charpentier, a liberal publisher, who commissioned him to paint Mme. Charpentier, who was herself a well known figure in the literary world, with her two children (plates 19 and 20). Through her he was introduced to the world of letters. He met such important writers as Mallarmé, Maupassant, Huysmans and, but only once, Turgenev. Although he was in a milieu that was not very much to his taste, it brought him what he desired – a number of commissions for portraits which augured well for a successful and financially rewarding career. Nevertheless, Renoir's real interests lay not in portraiture or society life and although he continued to paint portraits they were as few as were necessary to provide himself with an income.

It did not, however, prevent Renoir from maintaining contact with some of his wealthy clients. The Bérard family had a property near Dieppe and he went frequently to stay with them. In 1879 he felt sufficiently secure to marry and in 1881 made an extended trip to Italy lasting

PLATE 17
The Swing (1876)
Oil on canvas, 36¹/₄ x 28³/₄ inches (92 x 73cm)

This subject, a further study of the effects sunlight can produce, was painted around the same time as the Moulin de la Galette *(plate 15), in the garden of Renoir's house in the rue Cortot. The woman in the swing is reported to be Jeanne, a working-class girl from Montmartre, who appears elsewhere in Renoir's work. Her two friends and the small child are unidentified. The atmosphere of uncomplicated, calm enjoyment of the sun and conversation, the privacy of the group emphasized by the distant figures, makes the sense of reality palpable and the Impressionist identity of the work complete. It was at this time that Renoir was at his most intensely Impressionist, both in intention and technique. It is perhaps appropriate here to note a recurrent feature of Impressionist work – the absence of a determined spatial structure. If one considers the heads of the two men, the trunk of the tree and the foliage around them, although perfectly interpretable, they are not separately and spatially identified but seen in equal relationship to the picture plane, the paint surface. In relation to academic space structure, this is a dramatic and characteristic innovation found in all Impressionists at some stage in their work.*

the whole of the second half of the year when he painted and visited galleries with his new wife, Aline Charigot. She had for some years been his mistress and model and features in a number of his paintings, including *The Luncheon of the Boating Party* (c. 1880) and some of his nude studies. In Italy he was greatly attracted by Venice and its great Renaissance painters. He also visited the galleries in Florence, although the city failed to enchant him, and in Rome visited the great Raphael Stanze in the Vatican which had a profound influence on him and which affected all his later work.

On his return from Italy early in 1882, either as a result of the influence of the works of art that he had seen there or because his restless spirit needed new fields to explore, Renoir became increasingly dissatisfied with his own painting. He visited Cézanne at L'Estaque, who was in the process of developing a new pictorial architecture, and it is possible that this too promoted the idea of search and change in Renoir's philosophy. While still in Italy, in January 1882, he had visited the frescoes in Pompeii and then gone on to Palermo to ask Wagner's permission to paint him, to which Wagner claimed that he had never allowed anyone to paint him from life. Nevertheless, he permitted Renoir to come and Wagner sat for about 20 minutes before he pleaded tiredness and withdrew. The brief unfinished sketch, and a study made from it, remain a rare record of the great composer.

During that time Renoir had became increasingly convinced that Impressionism had led him astray, that the form of classicism he had encountered in fine painting in Italy, and the qualities that he discerned in Cézanne, were the direction that his art should take. His personal Impressionism was at an end. He had not exhibited in the Impressionist exhibitions of 1879, 1880 and 1881, although he did return with 25 works for the 1882 show, among which was a painting called *The Luncheon of the Boating Party* (plate 24).

It was around this time that Renoir began to show the first signs of an illness that would eventually cripple him. On the way back from Italy, in Marseille, he had caught a cold which turned to pneumonia, but on a doctor's advice had made a second visit to Algiers. On his return, he painted steadily for an exhibition arranged for April 1882 by Durand-Ruel and showed 70 works covering his painting career from 1870. The exhibition established his reputation and assured him that, provided he continued his Impressionist works, he had no need for concern for his financial future. Characteristically, it was at this point that Renoir abandoned Impressionism. At the end of 1883 he told Ambroise Vollard, dealer and friend of the independent group: 'I had come to the end of Impressionism and had arrived at a condition in which I did not know how to paint or draw. In a word, I was at an impasse.'

PLATE 18
Les Grands Boulevards (1875) below
Oil on canvas, 20½ x 25 inches (52.1 x 63.5cm)

The effect of Baron Haussmann's rebuilding of the centre of Paris, which included wide boulevards and large classical avenues of architecture, was to create an open city with streets lined with trees, illuminated in the wider spaces provided by the boulevards by full sunlight. It is a scene that Renoir has painted in a full Impressionist work, using the trees both as a source of vibrant colour and disguising the monotony, as Renoir saw it, of long classical façades.

PLATE 19
Madame Charpentier (1876–77)
Oil on canvas, 18 x 15 inches (46 x 38cm)

Georges Charpentier, soon after his meeting with Renoir, commissioned this rich and attractive portrait of his wife which in turn led the large painting of Madame Charpentier and her two children (plate 20). Renoir's intention of becoming a portrait-painter was much advanced by his contact with the family as Madame Charpentier was a noted society hostess who introduced Renoir to a number of important clients. That his inquisitive spirit led him in different directions is a characteristic of his life and the nature of his painting.

PLATE 20

Madame Charpentier and her Children
(1878)

Oil on canvas, 60²/₃ x 75 inches (154 x 190.5cm)

Renoir's meeting with Georges Charpentier, a successful Parisian publisher, seemed especially fortuitous since at this period in his life he was intending to become a portrait-painter as a way of making a living. He had already made a portrait of Jeanne Samary (plate 21), a well known actress and this, together with the commissions he received to paint members of the Charpentier family, set him well on the way to becoming a successful portraitist. He met Charpentier in 1876 and during this year or early in the next completed a strong and sympathetic portrait of Mme. Charpentier (plate 19). His use of deep-blue and near-black as a foil to the delicate colour and sensitive drawing of the head gives this work an air of authority and distinction which must have encouraged this larger commission for the mother with her children. Renoir did not show in the Impressionist exhibition of 1879, nor in the two following, but he was accepted for the Salon of 1879 with both the Samary and Charpentier family portraits.

Although there is the intimate air of a united family about the group painting, there are also the studied poses of the mother and children which were more academically acceptable to the Salon than to the independents of the Impressionist group. Had it not been for Renoir's own independent spirit of enquiry and experiment he might have developed into an effective portraitist but not the great master he was destined to become.

PLATE 21
Portrait of Jeanne Samary (1878)
Oil on canvas, 68 x 40½ inches (173 x 103cm)

This delightfully elegant portrait of a well known actress (who had also acted before as his model) was another of the paintings Renoir undertook, partly to encourage custom for the portraits from which he hoped to make a living. There is a pleasant frankness in the contrast of a figure who could well be a member of a higher social class and the insouciant freshness of a person who is a stage performer with all the implications associated with the profession at that time. Simultaneously both formal and informal, it already indicates that Renoir was right to expect a successful career as a portraitist. His portraits of both Jeanne Samary and Madame Charpentier and her children (plate 20) were accepted for the 1879 Salon.

During 1881 Renoir had painted a number of nudes and landscapes which presaged his conversion to a classical linear style, sometimes called his 'sharp' or 'harsh' period. Among these paintings is a seated nude bather which is an evident mixture of linear and Impressionist elements. Like many of such studies it is of his wife.

The year 1884 saw the avant garde's dismissal of both the realist tradition and Impressionism for the beginning of the next generation of young painters who, in May, and calling themselves 'Le Groupe des Indépendants', organized an exhibition. Although it was not successful and attracted little attention, it included work by Seurat and Signac who subsequently organized a new group, the 'Société des Artistes Indépendants', continuing the theme proposed by Degas for the first Impressionist exhibition and holding their first show in December. It was the beginning of the succession of movements which occurred from then until the 1930s throughout Europe. Not only had Impressionism been superseded but it was also old-hat – a new academicism. The Impressionist painters had ceased to be members of the avant garde and were now masters whose work was collected, whose prices correspondingly rose, and each of them now individually pursued their own solutions.

There was no Salon des Indépendants in 1885, but the following year the Seurat group held the second Salon des Indépendants and, symbolically perhaps, 1886 also saw the last, and eighth Impressionist exhibition take place. Organized by Berthe Morisot in consultation with Degas, it was simply called the '8ième Exposition de Peinture', at his insistence. He had never wished their exhibitions to be called *impressioniste*, preferring instead *indépendant*, but was pre-empted at the end by the up-and-coming generation.

Renoir's contribution to this new stage in the history of 19th-century French art was not inconsiderable. We have already noted a new linear structural basis to his painting of the nude bather. Another well known painting of this time is *Les Parapluies* (plate 32), in which elements of both his new linear and old Impressionist style are present; the new linear in the figure on the left and the old Impressionist in the figures on the right. The *Grandes Baigneuses* (plate 34) of 1887 represents the full expression of Renoir's linear, classical style as it had developed. If it is compared with the *Moulin de la Galette* (plate 15) of ten years earlier, his pictorial development from Impressionism is evident. Of course it will come as no surprise to learn that, having come to terms with and even shown enthusiasm for Renoir's 'Impressionism', both public and critics took his pictorial recidivism as a personal insult and were dismayed by the sharp coldness of his new direction. It was not until the earlier years of this century, when his whole work could be viewed, that his adventurous independent spirit could be fully appreciated.

PLATE 22
Portrait of Alphonsine Fournaise (1879)
Oil on canvas, 19²/₃ x 15³/₄ inches (50 x 40cm)

The daughter of the proprietor of the Restaurant Fournaise, the location for the Luncheon of the Boating Party (plate 24), *is the subject of this painting which includes a view along the Seine from the same balcony towards the rail bridge at Chatou. Originally it was thought to have been La Grenouillère. The rail bridge is yet another reference to the importance that all the Impressionists attached to the ubiquitous industrial development as an expression of modern civilization.*

But the stylistic changes were not yet over. Renoir returned for a time to his earlier Impressionist technique at the beginning of the 1890s, having realized that the harsh linear style did not really express his intention and during the decade a more luminous, softer feeling began to emerge in his painting, the expression of the contained volume being maintained but without clear linear definition. His subjects included landscapes, young girls – clothed and nude – and portraits of his family. His great friend Gustave Caillebotte died in 1894, leaving Renoir as his executor to arrange for Caillebotte's bequest of his collection to the nation to be accepted by the Louvre. The officials of the École des Beaux Arts, still suspicious of the new developments in painting and anxious to maintain their authority, refused to accept them. As a result, Renoir was obliged to spend much time and energy in tiresome bickering. In the end he was only partially successful, and 65 works were eventually accepted.

The late 1880s and early 1890s were an indeterminate

PLATE 23
Portrait of Stéphane Mallarmé (1824-98)
Oil on canvas, 19²/₃ x 15³/₄ inches (50 x 40cm)

Mallarmé was one of the important literary figures of 19th-century Paris, a poet and prose writer with a considerable reputation. He was a contemporary of the Impressionists, a close friend of Manet, Degas and Renoir and a strong apologist for the movement. He earned his living teaching English in various schools in Paris; while teaching at the Lycée Condorcet, he called on Manet every day. Mallarmé became an influential figure, not only through his writings, but also through the Tuesday soirées held at his flat in the rue de Rome where most of the Impressionists forgathered at one time or another. His eclogue, L'après-midi d'un faune, inspired Debussy's prélude. Mallarmé's poetry reflected a belief that it alone provided an authenticity to life on earth – the only reality (a theme later developed by the Existentialists) being the one in which one lives. This was a notion that was in sympathy with the Impressionist aim of immediacy of vision. The painting itself is a study in a style that succeeds Renoir's Impressionist period.

period for Renoir. His first son, Pierre, born in 1885 and his second, Jean, born in 1894, both became subjects of his painting as had been, and still was, Renoir's wife, Aline. He also painted a number of landscapes both in northern and southern France. In retrospect, it seems as though Renoir had not decided on a new direction but was exploring whether there were any possibilities in what he had already produced. Also, what had already been threatened was becoming a reality; he began to suffer attacks of arthritis in 1894.

The onset of what was to become a serious disability and which was to greatly inhibit the continuation of Renoir's painting programme resulted in his decision, in 1903, to move the family to Cagnes-sur-Mer on the French Riviera where he bought a house and land in 1907, Les Collettes. There were times when he was unable to paint and was eventually to spend much of his time in a wheel-chair when his brushes had to be strapped to his hand. By 1912, he was partly paralysed. His third son, Claude (Coco), had been born in 1901 and quickly became another subject for this his late style.

It might be expected that as a result of his illness the major achievements of his painting would be over. Nothing could have been further from the truth because it is now recognized that when all the stress and soul-searching was over, when his energies had to be carefully husbanded, his experience, technique and range supported

him in a last great period of nudes and bathing groups which put him among the young moderns of the 20th century. He died in Cagnes on 3 December 1919.

It should be noted that in his last years, with the aid of assistants, Renoir created some sculptures of which a large nude, *Venus*, is his best known. Much like Degas, who was at the same time suffering from a serious and continuing deterioration of his sight, Renoir turned to sculpture when he was hardly able to control his painting hand and, with the aid of assistants who modelled the clay to his directions, created a number of important works. Like Degas, his subjects were his own personal favourites, members of his family and nudes. It is interesting to note that he called what is actually a standing nude study, *Venus Victorious* (plate 45) – an indication of the continuing classical identification intended to gain credibility with the academics; underlying Renoir's independent spirit there always remained a perhaps grudging, but nonetheless real respect for the Salon.

A study of the illustrations in this book will indicate the variety of styles and variations in quality of Renoir's *oeuvre*. There is no doubt that he was an important and influential Impressionist painter, responsible not only for some of the most memorable works of the movement, but was also an exploratory painter for whom Impressionism was not enough. Since Renoir lived into this century, with

Continued on page 53

PLATE 24
The Luncheon of the Boating Party
(1880–81)

Oil on canvas, 51¼ x 68 inches (130 x 173cm)

As with Le Moulin de la Galette *(plate 15) and others, Renoir painted works which summarized his attitude, even encapsulated it at various stages of his career in major representative works, in* tours de force, *and this painting brings Renoir's Impressionist period to a close. The painting is located on the first-floor balcony of the Restaurant Fournaise overlooking the Seine on the island of Chiard, near Chatou, and was a favourite meeting place for boatmen, poets and intellectuals. Although the Impressionist method and treatment was not lost to Renoir and appeared later on different occasions, the specific identification was at an end. As usual, some of Renoir's friends are among those depicted and a model, soon to become his wife, Aline Charigot, is seated to the left with a little dog looking remarkably like the griffon in an earlier work (plate 6). The other girl at the table is another favourite model, Angèle, of singularly colourful reputation and Caillebotte sits astride the chair in the foreground. Renoir confessed to having contemplated the subject for some time and although he was just 40 claimed, 'I am not getting any younger and did not want to put off this little feast.' It is almost a statement of projected change. It is likely that the design was made during the summer of 1880 while Renoir was staying with Mère Fournaise at Croissy. He exhibited the work at the seventh Impressionist show of 1882 after a gap of a number of years.*

The composition is an interesting balance between the two halves created by the diagonal from bottom left to top right. Most of the figures are concentrated in the lower half and a vista is pierced through the foliage in the upper, while the striped awning holds the eye within the picture. Although the figures are tightly packed, they appear to recess comfortably into the near distance; but it may noticed that to contrive this, Renoir has given the near table a lower eye-level than the other, thus allowing more to be seen of the background. The varied twisting turns of the figures within this structure reveal Renoir's pictorial maturity. While not as well known as the Moulin, *this is another undoubted masterpiece.*

PLATE 25
Dance at Bougival (1882–83) opposite
Oil on canvas, 71²/₃ x 38¹/₂ inches (182 x 98cm)

PLATE 26
Dance in Town (1883) above
Oil on canvas, 70⁷/₈ x 35¹/₂ inches (180 x 90cm)

PLATE 27
Dance in the Country (1883) above right
Oil on canvas, 70⁷/₈ x 35¹/₂ (180 x 90cm)

Dance in the Country *is a large vertical canvas, almost
life-sized, and one of two panels Renoir painted as
companion pieces, the other being* Dance in Town. *A third
painting,* Dance at Bougival, *completes three studies of
dancing in different moods. The third looks back to the
boating scene while the other two seem to be designed as
decorative panels in a new and harder linear style, presaging a
new 'harsh' method which Renoir developed for a short
period. The male model for all three paintings was his friend
Paul Lhôte and the girl in the country and town panels was
Maria Clémentine who later became a well known painter,
Suzanne Valadon, and the mother of Maurice Utrillo.*

PLATE 28
Renoir with his family

PLATE 29 opposite
Renoir at work in his studio with model

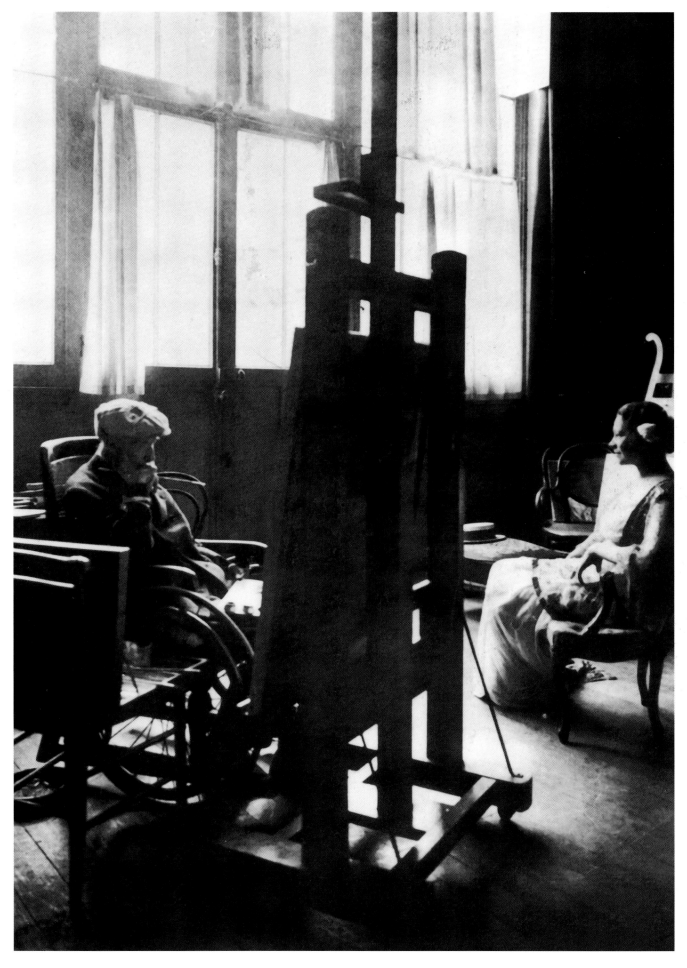

PLATE 30 left

The exterior of Renoir's house, Les Collettes, at Cagnes-sur-Mer, photographed in 1908

PLATE 31 above

Renoir's studio, showing his easel and wheel-chair

PLATE 32

Les Parapluies (Umbrellas) 1881–86) opposite

Oil on canvas, 70⁷/₈ x 45¹/₄ inches (180 x 115cm)

PLATE 33

In the Luxembourg Gardens (1883) below

Oil on canvas, 25¹/₄ x 20⁷/₈ inches (64 x 53cm)

Renoir's independence of mind, mentioned a number of times, had always prevented him from being irrevocably locked into the Impressionist mould and after 1880 he was in search of a new range of expression, influenced by visits to Cézanne, the south of France, Algeria and Italy – notably to Venice. The Umbrellas, *begun in 1881 and painted over a period, coincided with the beginning of a change and the painting clearly reveals this. One element in that change was that Renoir decided to work mostly in the studio rather than en plein-air, describing outdoor painting as too complicated, demanding constant compromise, and this*

painting – a dense grouping of figures – was obviously not only an opportunity to work in his studio but almost a necessity. The result, over the time it took to paint it, is a mixture of mainly Impressionist methods on the right, particularly the child with the hoop and her family, and the strongly defined figures on the left-hand side. So clearly are forms drawn that voids become solids, as in the interior of the basket or the undersides of the umbrellas. It is the beginning of the so-called 'harsh' style of defined form and carefully gradated colour areas. There is, for instance, in the two little girls on the right a softness and charm not evident in the girl with the basket.

The small study In the Luxembourg Gardens *painted at that time is also clear evidence of the struggle for a new development that Renoir was undergoing at the time. Rather than a single unified composition, it is a group of episodes related to the major work and suggesting that the larger work is located in the gardens.*

Continued from page 43

a growing reputation, his influence on the early 20th-century pictorial philosophy is significant, particularly his later work which perhaps not surprisingly follows something of a similar course to that of his longer-living contemporaries, Degas and Monet. Monet, like Degas, almost lost his sight in his later years, and the work of the three painters all showed an inevitable loss of detail and physical precision in their last years; but their knowledge, experience and determination meant that they could still produce work of the highest sensitivity, transcending their physical disabilities. Monet was a difficult man in his later years, a recluse and a domestic martinet. Degas also became reclusive, his sharp tongue and reserved nature a vestige of the way he viewed his position in society, and always setting him apart. He was not a convivial person.

But Renoir was different. His was a kind, generous and happy nature, rooted in a typically French artisan/bourgeois character – what might be described as a nice man. An appropriate anecdote ends his story. He was once asked to confirm that a painting ascribed to him was a forgery in order that the forger might be convicted. On learning that the man was wretched and destitute, he painted over the picture, thus authenticating it and saving the man from prosecution.

It is possible with Renoir's work to divide it into the periods of stylistic change, since these changes were

relatively dramatic and hence identifiable. They are: the early years; the Impressionist period; the sharp/harsh period; the radiant/iridescent period; resolution at Cagnes.

PLATE 34
Les Grandes Baigneuses (The Bathers)
(1884–1887) previous pages
Oil on canvas, 45¹/₂ x 67 inches (116 x 170cm)

Renoir worked on this subject over a period of two or three years making many studies, sketches of details, and changes in composition in preparatory versions. Some of the figure studies he made became individual works. Many influences can be discerned in this work: the classical inspiration led him to Ingres and Raphael (whose work he had admired in Rome) and the clarity of fresco and its simplicity of paint and colour. The lively poses were derived from Girardon's work at Versailles. However, the spirit of the work is essentially Renoir and the style 'harsh' – his période aigre masterpiece. Renoir made the following comments: 'After three years of experimentation, The Bathers, which I considered my master-work, was finished. I sent it to an exhibition – and what a trouncing I got! This time, everybody, Huysmans in the forefront, agreed that I was really sunk; some even said I was irresponsible. And God knows how I laboured over it.' Perhaps he should not have been surprised: when people do the unexpected they are often thought to have gone off the rails! But different as it is from Renoir's previous Impressionist work, it is nevertheless a great creative expression of classical joie de vivre.

PLATE 35
Montagne Sainte-Victoire (1889)
Oil on canvas, 20⁷/₈ x 25¹/₄ inches (53 x 64.1cm)

During Renoir's travels in 1889, he rented a house in Aix-en-Provence belonging to Maxime Conil, Cézanne's brother-in-law, and with Cézanne painted the same subjects from the same viewpoint at the same time. The tight architectural structure of Cézanne's painting of one of his favourite subjects, the dominating form of the great mountain, is not however repeated in Renoir's version which carries residual evidence of Impressionism but in which the forms are more volumetrically constructed than they would have been during his Impressionist period.

PLATE 36
Madame de Bonnières (1889) opposite
Oil on canvas, 46 x 35 inches (117 x 89cm)

A delicate but unconvincing portrait with less than accurate drawing, this seems to be more of an uninvolved portrait commission which reveals how difficult portraiture can become when all the abilities and sympathies are not totally engaged.

PLATE 37
The Rambler (1895) detail
Oil on canvas, 24 x 19²/₃ inches (61 x 50cm)

When clearly engaged and enthusiastic, Renoir is likely to bring power and originality to an open-air subject, even when using a model who has in all probability hardly set foot outside Montmartre and has been painted in a studio. This work was completed after both the Impressionist and 'harsh' stages in Renoir's career and shows an engaging assurance, needing only a vague sense of the open-air in the background and a strong walking-stick to establish the subject. The firmness and clarity of the drawing show Renoir in his maturity before physically afflicted when in 1888 his face became partially paralysed and made firm linear painting excessively and progressively difficult.

PLATE 38
Berthe Morisot with her Daughter
(1894) detail
Sketch in pastel, 23¹/₄ x 17⁷/₈ inches (59 x 45.5cm)

Berthe Morisot (1841–95) was one of the most intelligent and talented of the Impressionist group. She was greatly admired by Renoir who painted her a number of times. After her early death at the age of 54, her daughter, Julie Manet, became Renoir's ward.

PLATE 39
Bather with Long Hair (c. 1895) opposite
Oil on canvas, 32¹/₄ x 25¹/₂ inches (82 x 65cm)

Comparison of this painting with Les Grandes Baigneuses *(plate 34) indicates that Renoir had abandoned his 'harsh' style for a more delicate and, in some ways, Impressionist method. Edges are no longer sharply defined and the forms are fully rounded with a sympathetic painting of flesh in Renoir's highly personal technique. The vague indication of location – foliage and water means bather – concentrates the attention on the young and rounded nude figure which Renoir delighted in painting, often using the same model for different paintings and only altering the hair. The pose, and the absence of pubic hair, indicates that Renoir had a classical image in mind.*

PLATE 40
Portrait of Claude (Coco) Renoir (1905-08)
Oil on canvas, 21$^7/_8$ x 18$^1/_2$ inches (55.5 x 47cm)

PLATE 41
The Clown (Portrait of Claude Renoir)
1909 opposite
Oil on canvas, 47$^1/_4$ x 30$^1/_3$ inches (120 x 77cm)

Renoir used his whole household as models and most of his female staff for his nude studies. These two paintings of his third son Claude, *nicknamed 'Coco' and born in 1901, were separated by a few years. While the smaller painting of the younger child is a relaxed, simple study, the second of Coco dressed as a clown was done after an altercation between painter and model. His female models showed remarkable acquiescence in response to Renoir's strict demands for absolute stillness, but the children objected to any prolonged period of restraint. Coco took firmly against the costume, particularly the white stockings, claiming they itched. Renoir threatened a beating to no avail and was eventually driven to bribery in the form of a box of paints and a train-set. Claude still looks unhappy and one can imagine Renoir still seething away.*

PLATE 42
Portrait of Ambroise Vollard (1908) opposite
Oil on canvas, 31¹/₈ x 25¹/₂ inches (79 x 65cm)

*Vollard, the Impressionist dealer, was painted by most of them
and later became the dealer for many of the early artists of the
20th century including Picasso, Matisse and Chagall. This is
Renoir's first portrait of him examining a small statuette by the
sculpture Aristide Maillol (1861-1944). He later (1917) painted
him disguised as a bull-fighter. Vollard was responsible for Renoir
turning to sculpture when arthritis inhibited his painting.*

PLATE 43
Portrait of Mme. Edwards (Misia Sert)
(1904) detail above
Oil on canvas, 36¹/₄ x 28³/₄ inches (92 x 73cm)

*A late commissioned portrait, this painting reveals Renoir's
assurance and authority in the broad handling of paint.*

PLATE 44
A Terrace at Cagnes (1905)
Oil on canvas, 18 x 21⅞ inches (46 x 55.5cm)

*Renoir visited Cagnes-sur-Mer on the shores of the
Mediterranean east of Cannes in the winter of 1899. Following
this visit he formed a strong attachment to the area and as
rheumatism increasingly attacked his hands began the search for a
place to which he could retreat and continue painting his
landscapes and the female nude studies that increasingly
preoccupied him. From the beginning of the 20th century he had
spent an increasing number of winters at Cagnes, and in 1907
bought a plot of hillside with an old farmhouse known as Les
Collettes on which he built a house and studio. His land faced
the small ancient hill-town of Hautes Cagnes, and the painting
illustrated here is a view of a terrace on the outskirts of that town,
completed before he bought Les Collettes. The deterioration of
control and refinement, the result of his crippled hands and
diminished eyesight, are apparent in this canvas, as is also his
determination to continue working.*

PLATE 45
Venus Victorious (1914) page 68
Bronze, over life-size

*Venus is here depicted holding the golden apple awarded to her by
Paris, a mythological theme that Renoir found fascinating in his
later life and made the subject of a number of works. His
sculptures, due to the crippling effects of arthritis, were actually
made by his assistant/partner Richard Guino who was introduced
to him by Ambroise Vollard.*

PLATE 46
Mother and Child (c.1916, cast 1927) page 69
Bronze, height 21¼ inches (54cm)

*A study of Madame Renoir nursing her first child Pierre.
Executed after her death in 1915, it is possible that it was a
study for a larger commemorative piece to be placed on her tomb.*

PLATE 47
M. & Mme. Bernheim de Villers (1910)
opposite
Oil on canvas, $31^7/_8$ x $25^3/_4$ inches (81 x 65.5cm)

A commissioned portrait of the art dealer Gaston and his wife
Suzanne when Renoir was at the height of his success.

PLATE 48
Gabrielle with a Rose
Oil on canvas, $21^7/_8$ x $18^1/_2$ inches (55.5 x 47cm)

Gabrielle Renard was a frequent model as well as the family
servant and this study shows her in a semi-transparent blouse
with barely covered breasts toying with a rose in her hair. A
dreamily erotic image

PLATE 49

Portrait of Mlle. Françoise (c.1915) opposite

Oil on canvas, 25$\frac{1}{2}$ x 20$\frac{7}{8}$ inches (65 x 53cm)

Similar in character to the previous painting, this is one of which there is another similar and the sitter appears, like Gabrielle, in a 'sweet disorder of the dress'. Renoir was not averse to changing details of colour and scale if it coincided with his feeling for the image he wished to achieve.

PLATE 50

The Bathers (c.1918–19) overleaf

Oil on canvas, 43$\frac{1}{3}$ x 63 inches (110 x 160cm)

This painting, sometimes, if surprisingly known as The Nymphs, is the most significant of Renoir's baigneuses, a theme he had pursued through most of his painting career. The earlier Grandes Baigneuses of 1884–87 (plate 34) was in a sharply defined linear form – his harsh period – whereas this is painted with soft reverence for form and not edges. It should be remembered that when he painted this work he had for some years been crippled with arthritis in his hands and was now unable to walk. He was living in Cagnes, his wife had died, and the world was at war. The avant garde art of the day had already spawned Fauvism, Cubism, Futurism, German Expressionism and Surrealism was

incipient. The work on this painting must have begun about the time of the Armistice of 11 November 1918 and possibly was even inspired by the personal culmination of Renoir's own career – at all events his son Jean thought so. Compared with earlier work on the same theme so popular with Renoir, it reveals a new depth of spirit, a surface sunlit calm, almost an idyllic presentation of the physicality of human female sensuality in a lush verdant world. For this work he employed a new 16-year-old red-haired model, Dédée Hessling, who after Renoir's death became Jean's wife. There is something movingly appropriate in the finale to Renoir's career.

As frequently happens, the painting was not appreciated by all at the time and many did not admire his later paintings, particularly his nudes. Mary Cassatt, the American Impressionist, had described them in 1913 as 'awful pictures ... of enormously fat red women with small heads'. But if looked at with sympathetic and understanding eyes they become images of great pictorial power, full of the grandeur of human sensuality without its darker side.

It is the core of Renoir's oeuvre that whatever his subject, whether he was attempting a classical subject or the most intimate personal study, his joy in living nature and devotion to his art inspired some of the most memorable images of the 19th century.

━━━ ACKNOWLEDGEMENT ━━━

The Publishers wish to thank the following for providing photographs, and for permission to reproduce copyright material. While every effort has been made to trace and acknowledge copyright-holders, we wish to apologize should any omissions have been made.

Photograph of Pierre-Auguste Renoir
Larousse Archives/Giraudon, Paris
The Painter Lacoeur in the Forest of Fontainebleau
São Paulo Museum of Art/Giraudon, Paris
Portrait of Frédéric Bazille
Louvre/Giraudon, Paris
Lise with a Parasol
Folkwang Museum, Essen/Giraudon, Paris
Boy with a Cat
Musée d'Orsay/Giraudon, Paris
Bather with her Griffon
São Paulo Museum of Art/Giraudon, Paris
La Grenouillère
Pushkin Museum, Moscow/Giraudon, Paris
Portrait of Claude Monet
Musée Marmottan/Giraudon, Paris
Portrait of Claude Monet
Musée d'Orsay/Giraudon, Paris
La Loge
Courtaud Institute Galleries/Bridgeman/Giraudon, Paris
Path Winding Upwards through Tall Grass
Musée d'Orsay/Giraudon, Paris
Woman Reading
Musée d'Orsay/Giraudon, Paris
Young Woman Wearing a Veil
Musée d'Orsay/Giraudon, Paris
Nude Study: The Effect of Sunlight
Musée d'Orsay/Giraudon, Paris
Le Moulin de la Galette
Musée d'Orsay/Giraudon, Paris
Parisian Women Dressed as Algerians
National Museum of Western Art, Tokyo
The Swing
Musée d'Orsay/Giraudon, Paris
Les Grands Boulevards
Philadelphia Museum of Art.
The Henry P. McIlhenny Collection in memory of Frances P. McIlhenny
Madame Charpentier
Musée d'Orsay/Lauros/Giraudon, Paris
Madame Charpentier and her Children
The Metropolitan Museum of Art, New York
Portrait of Jeanne Samary
The Hermitage Museum, St Petersburg/Giraudon, Paris
Portrait of Alphonsine Fournaise
Musée d'Orsay/Giraudon, Paris
Portrait of Stéphane Mallarmé
Château de Versailles/Giraudon, Paris
The Luncheon of the Boating Party
Phillips' Collection/Giraudon, Paris
Dance at Bougival
Boston Museum of Fine Arts

Dance in Town
Musée d'Orsay
Dance in the Country (see opposite)
Musée d'Orsay/Giraudon, Paris
Renoir with his family (photograph)
Hulton Getty
Renoir at work in his studio with model (photograph)
Hulton Getty
Renoir's House at Cagnes (photograph)
Hulton Getty
Renoir's Studio
Hulton Getty
Renoir's Studio, showing his easel and wheelchair
Lauros/Giraudon, Paris
An exterior of his house Les Collettes, at Cagnes, taken in 1908.
Lauros/Giraudon, Paris
Les Parapluies (Umbrellas)
The National Gallery, London/Bridgeman/Giraudon, Paris
In the Luxembourg Gardens
Private Collection, Geneva/Giraudon, Paris
Les Grandes Baigneuses (The Bathers)
Pennsylvania Museum of Fine Art, Philadelphia/
Bridgeman/Giraudon, Paris
Montagne Sainte-Victoire
Yale University Art Gallery, New Haven, Connecticut.
The Katherine Ordway Collection
Madame de Bonnières
Musée du Petit-Palais/Lauros/Giraudon, Paris
The Rambler
Musée des Beaux-Arts André Malraux, Le Havre/Giraudon, Paris
Berthe Morisot with her Daughter
Musée du Petit-Palais/Giraudon, Paris
Bather with Long Hair
Musée de l'Orangerie/Lauros/Giraudon, Paris
Portrait of Claude (Coco) Renoir
São Paulo Museum of Art/Giraudon, Paris
The Clown (Portrait of Claude Renoir)
Musée de l'Orangerie/Lauros/Giraudon, Paris
Portrait of Ambroise Vollard
Courtaud Institute Galleries/Bridgeman/Giraudon, Paris
Portrait of Mme. Edwards (Misia Sert)
Giraudon, Paris
A Terrace at Cagnes
Bridgestone Museum of Art, Tokyo/Giraudon, Paris
Venus Victorious
Renoir Museum, Les Collettes, Cagnes-sur-Mer/Lauros/Giraudon, Paris
Mother and Child
Renoir Museum, Les Collettes, Cagnes-sur-Mer/Lauros/Giraudon, Paris
M. & Mme. Bernheim de Villers
Musée d'Orsay/Lauros/Giraudon, Paris
Gabrielle with a Rose
Musée d'Orsay/Giraudon, Paris
Portrait of Mlle Françoise
Musée de l'Orangerie/Lauros/Giraudon, Paris/Knudsens
The Bathers
Musée d'Orsay

Claude
Monet

Trewin Copplestone

List of Plates

PLATE 1
Woman from Normandy in Profile
(c. 1856–57) opposite left
Black chalk, $9^7/_8$ x $6^1/_4$ inches (25 x 16cm)

PLATE 2
Young Dandy with Monocle and Cigar
(c. 1856–57) right
Black chalk with colour crayon, $9^7/_8$ x $6^1/_4$ inches
(25 x 16cm)

These two examples of Monet's early artistic interest as well as of his financial enterprise, made when he was about 15, show him to be a caricaturist beyond normal expectation and indeed his drawing at that time also showed academic ability. This form of portrait illustration was popular in the 19th century and such figures as Spy achieved a considerable reputation from similar treatment of famous figures of the day. Nevertheless, the influence of Boudin soon redirected Monet to more serious painting.

The Impressionist revolution, one of the most dramatically successful and influential developments in the character of Western art since the beginning of the Renaissance, is encapsulated in the life and work of Claude Monet, recognized universally as the quintessential figure of the movement. The course of Impressionism is delineated through Monet's working life which covers the whole of the latter part of the 19th century and up to the second decade of the 20th century. Monet and Impressionism are so interrelated that it seems at times that he must be the only Impressionist, so much does he personify its characteristics and qualities. His long life encompassed many domestic and personal difficulties during which he struggled to enlarge his art. The result is a consistent if changing development which ended with a series of massive panels epitomizing his philosophy and becoming the greatest single monument to the success of the Impressionist movement.

Of course, a whole art movement cannot be encompassed in the work of one artist. The wider the accepted generic coverage of any movement or period, the greater the number of artists that may be included and appropriately identified. In, for instance, a broadly inclusive term such as 'Renaissance', many artists of different nationalities and pictorial intention over a long time span may be included, with each contributing something significantly different to the general classification. When the grouping is numerically small, spans only a short period of time, consists mainly of one nationality, and with few formative figures as is the case with Impressionism, the contribution of each individual artist will materially affect the perceived character of the movement. For this reason, it is essential to be clear which artists may properly be included before one can establish the parameters of the movement.

With Monet at the heart, we may confidently claim Renoir, Sisley, Pissarro as original participants and determinants while Degas, although always claiming to be an independent and not liking the term Impressionist, was clearly associated and contributary. It has been said that any attempted definition of Impressionism which definitely excluded him would be inadequate although ultimately it has to be recognized that few of his paintings are even approximate to the evident intention and character of Monet's work. Another artist usually included in the Impressionist net is Manet, eight years older than Monet and the recognized leader of the group of independent painters from which the Impressionists emerged. His association is even more questionable than Degas'. He did not exhibit in the first Impressionist show in 1874 but he was a friend of Monet's. His painting philosophy and practice was never close to that of the Impressionists and he is now regarded more as an influence than as a participant. Other painters are also usually included, such

as Cézanne, who through Pissarro certainly had a short connection; Bazille, who died in the Franco-Prussian War of 1870 before the first 'Impressionist' exhibition; Van Gogh and Gauguin, inaccurately, but because of their association with the group; and a number of others because of a perceived Impressionist character in their work, such as the two sculptors Auguste Rodin and Medardo Rosso, and even others because they exhibited in the first Impressionist exhibition. Thus, in attempting to identify Impressionism and its artists, it is essential to identify what it is first, and we are confronted with a chicken and egg situation; an unresolvable problem. It has usually been helpful to examine Monet's contribution as an *a priori* situation.

Claude-Oscar Monet was born in the rue Laffitte, Paris on 14 November 1840, into the *petit bourgeoisie*. His father and uncles were all grocers and ship chandlers, living comfortably without ambition or wide interests and except for one aunt, who was an amateur painter, the family had no interest in the arts. When Monet was five, the family moved to Le Havre, a port on the north coast of France at the estuary of the Seine, and his father entered a partnership with his brother-in-law, a well-to-do

ship's chandler. Monet was unhappy at school, learned little and whenever possible spent his time on the beaches and cliffs or in boats on the water. It was at this time that his interest in the movement of water began and, indeed, with all nature, which remained with him throughout his long life. Indeed, most of the characteristics that he revealed in his mature life were already evident in the child. He was independent, in little need of praise or social approbation, irreligious and concerned only with what he learned from his own experience.

Perhaps most fortunately for him, he was stimulated by antagonism and adversity, both of which he was to experience early in his working life as a painter. On the other hand, he was self-indulgent – some said he ate enough for four ordinary appetites – could be vindictive and taciturn, and was crafty and manipulative with money. When only 15, he was selling caricatures of locals for 20 francs in the small stationery and framing shop in Le Havre which had been owned by the painter Eugène Boudin. He met Boudin, who was a landscape painter of the local coastal scenery and who, importantly for Monet's development, painted *en plein-air* – on site in the open-air; Boudin quickly transmitted his love of the coast which he

PLATE 3
Photograph of Monet (1913)

PLATE 4
Trophies of the Hunt (1862) opposite
Oil on canvas, 41 x 29¹/₂ inches (104 x 75cm)

This early work, painted when Monet was still studying at Gleyre's atelier, is an indication of the academically based influence under which he produced his first works. It is painted in the traditional tonal structure and representational presentation which was the only valued approach at that time. It was against this restrictive practice and exhibitionist intention that the young painters who later became the independent group, of which Monet was a member, rebelled. The values of this painting indicate that Monet already had control of his technique and was capable of academic draughtsmanship, despite the short training that he had received. It may not be an inspiring work, but it is clearly competent. Gleyre, commenting on one of Monet's paintings, observed 'Not bad! Not bad at all, that thing there!'

knew so intimately to Monet. Boudin himself had been encouraged to paint by some of his customers, painters who themselves had an influence in Monet's life; Thomas Couture, a well known academician, with whom Manet was a pupil for six years, Jean-François Millet, a painter of *genre* subjects of peasant scenes of pathos and simplicity, and Constant Troyon, a painter of animals – particularly cattle – in quiet landscapes.

Painting out-of-doors with oil paint was not usual or very practical until the convenient means of transporting the paints in tubes was introduced in the 1840s. Boudin was a determined practitioner who convinced Monet that it was essential to capture 'one's first impression'. This was the one essential principle that guided Monet, and was perhaps the subconscious reason that he called his painting, in the first exhibition of the independent group in 1874, *Impression: Sunrise* and Impressionists became the name by which the group was subsequently known. Louis Le Roy, a well known critic, wrote a review of the exhibition which he entitled 'The Exhibition of the Impressionists', not the name that the group had chosen nor did it represent the content of the exhibitors' work.

In May 1859, Monet visited Paris, went to the Salon, and admired the work of the Barbizon painters Daubigny and Troyon. He also attended the Académie Suisse where he met Pissarro and visited the Brasserie des Martyrs, where the Realist group foregathered around Courbet.

During the winter he saw a number of Delacroix's paintings at a loan exhibition. In the autumn of 1860 he was called up for military service and chose to serve in Algeria 'because of the sky'; he was excited by the light and colour he found there. He was, however, sent home on sick leave in 1862 and his family bought him out of the army so that he never completed his military service. In the summer of the same year, while painting on the coast with Boudin, he met Johan Barthold Jongkind, a Dutch landscape and seascape *plein-air* painter who worked mainly in France, anticipating Monet's later practice of painting the same subjects in different atmospheric conditions. Thus, at the beginning of his professional life, Monet had already been introduced to the two features which became the central foundation of his art, and thus, of Impressionism.

Monet returned to Paris in 1862 and, though he had been advised by Troyon to study with Couture, joined the atelier of Charles Gleyre. It is interesting to speculate what the effect on Monet – and on Impressionism – would have been had he chosen Couture. Gleyre was a celebrated and much admired painter and teacher. Although Monet was dissatisfied with the teaching, Gleyre was actually one of the more liberal and popular masters in Paris. In his atelier, Monet met Renoir, Sisley and Bazille – all of whom became part of the independent group when later formed. Bazille was an out-of-doors painter and

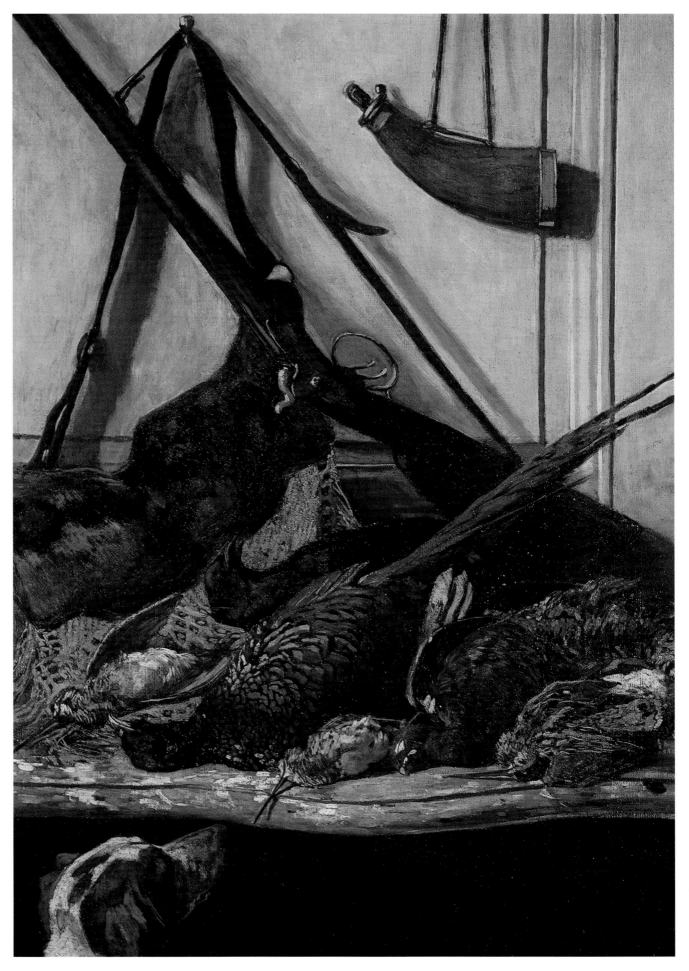

an important member of the group who is not as well known as the others since, as noted above, he was killed in the Franco-Prussian war of 1870 before the first Impressionist show.

The year 1863 was seminal in the development of the independent painters. In December of that year, Gleyre closed his studio – an almost symbolic event since it established the professional beginnings of the young independent students from his atelier. Even more significant to them in its immediate effect was the exhibition at the Louvre, from 15 May for a month, of the Salon des Refusés. This exhibition was staged on the command of Napoleon III that the paintings refused by the Salon itself should be shown in order to reveal, by contrast, the superiority of the Salon artists. Among the paintings of the *refusés* was Manet's *Déjeuner sur l'herbe* (above), which was the cause of a scandal since one of the figures in the painting was a naked female, accompanied by two elegantly dressed gentlemen. She looks boldly out of the picture as if defying censure and, incidentally, uncomfortably turning all viewers into unwitting voyeurs. This was all much too real for the *haut monde* and the critics, but for the young eager artists, already excited by the work of Delacroix, it was a clarion call to revolt. Although not at all what Manet had intended, he reluctantly became the leader of the avant garde and their meeting place became his favourite Café Guerbois.

Delacroix also died in 1863 and the admiration with which he was regarded by Monet and his friends was the inspiration for a new start, an artistic revolution. The reverence for the sturdy 'painterly' Romanticism of Delacroix himself even diminished and the classical, historicist and Romantic elements of the Salon were attacked by the young independents under the new banner of Realism, inspired by Courbet, who provides another strand in the developing artistic convictions of the nascent Impressionists. Gustave Courbet was born at Ornans, studied at Besançon and Paris, but was dismissive of tuition and was largely self-taught. He chose for his subjects landscapes and the everyday conditions of poor peasants he knew in his native village. In 1850, his painting *Burial at Ornans*, and exhibited at the Salon, caused a sensation, and was attacked on the grounds that the 30 figures represented combined to give an unreal view of a village ceremony, presenting the clergy as cynical and the peasants as degraded and brutal. Courbet himself had intended to give a sincere and sympathetic view of the villagers with whom he had grown up. His opposition to the false posturing of later Romantics and his scornful view of the whole academic training process revealed an independence which was an inspiration to the whole generation of young painters.

Courbet insisted that only the actual, tangible objects which existed in a real world, without imaginative

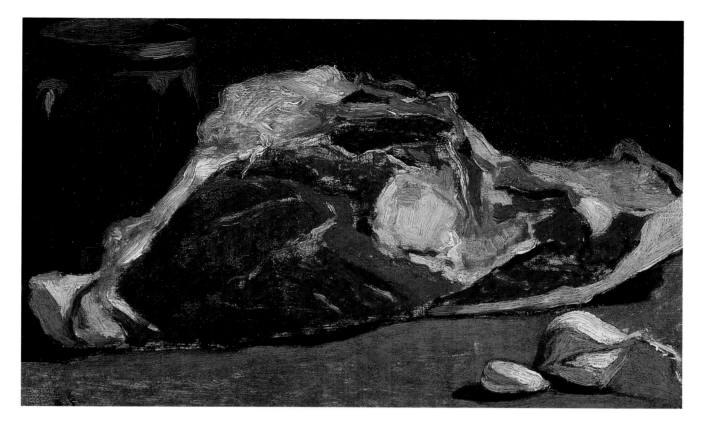

embellishment, idealization or alteration in the presentation of any subject, was acceptable. Monet and his friends from Gleyre's academy, Sisley, Renoir and Bazille were fully in sympathy with this view which was inherently part of the developing aesthetic of the age of Zola, Baudelaire and Balzac. Monet's response was, in a number of still-life paintings of the 1860s, to paint simple everyday objects, such as a single lamb chop or a couple of eggs with diligent vision and craftsmanship. Although of an inferior technical quality, Cézanne was also painting similar subjects at this time.

After the débâcle of the Salon des Refusés of 1863, which was not repeated, the Salon became the principal exhibition to which most painters, including the independents, were obliged to submit if they wished to show their work, and it is important to recognize that it ceased to be exclusively the outlet for academic exercises and began increasingly to accept the work of independents such as Boudin, Jongkind and Courbet, whose gold medal in 1849 meant that he was no longer subject to jury selection. In 1865 Monet submitted for the first time, and both his paintings were accepted and well regarded. 'The two marines of M. Monet are unquestionably the best in the exhibition,' declared one critic and when one recalls that Monet was then only 25 it must be regarded as an early success. His success was repeated in the Salon of 1866. He had painted a large *Déjeuner sur l'herbe*,

PLATE 5
Édouard Manet's Déjeuner sur l'herbe
(1863) detail opposite
Oil on canvas, 84½ x 106¼ inches (215 x 270cm)

PLATE 6
Still-Life: The Joint of Beef (1864) detail
above
Oil on canvas, 9 x 13 inches (24 x 33cm)

Monet undertook a number of small studies of grouped objects, particularly (as here) of meats and vegetables. As artificially arranged objects, as nature morte *rather than living nature, they allowed him to concentrate on the intrinsic character of the objects he was exploring. The resulting work has some of the quality of surprise and originality that already suggests that Monet was not content to follow a traditional painting career. It has also been noted that these paintings owe much to Chardin, whose still-life paintings are among the most admired legacies of 18th-century French art.*

PLATE 7
The Walkers (Study for Déjeuner sur l'herbe) 1865
Oil on canvas, 59 x 47¼ inches (150 x 120cm)

The Salon des Refusés of 1863 was a watershed for the young painters of independent mind through the scandal provided by Manet's Déjeuner sur l'herbe *(plate 5) and Monet was inspired to make his own version of the subject for the Salon of 1865 (plate 8). He was not able to complete it in time; he had intended a large scale work, approximately 5ft x 20ft (4.5m high by 6m wide), and in fact never did complete it. But he did make a number of studies for it, of which this is one, and did paint a smaller section for the Salon. He was in the first stages of his affair with Camille Doncieux and she modelled the female figures while a painter friend posed for the male figures, in this study, Frédéric Bazille, who was killed in the Franco-Prussian War. Monet's intention was different from Manet's. He wished to create a sense of the reality of the sunlit scene in which a picnic could properly take place.*

influenced by Manet, which he intended to show but, unable to complete it in time, painted, in four days, a life-sized portrait of his mistress and future wife, Camille Doncieux, which, with others of his works, was enthusiastically received. Despite this *succès d'estime* he was not selling his work and after a serious quarrel his family disowned him and withdrew their financial support.

Astonishingly, after such success, Monet only exhibited in the Salon twice more. The authorities, in the form of Count Nieuwerkerke, the Imperial Director of Fine Arts, recognized that the new group, with Monet as a prominent figure, was a threat to the academicians' continued dominance of the Salon so that, in 1867, one of Monet's important paintings *Women in the Garden* (plate 9) was rejected. Monet never forgot the slight and many years later, when the government wished to purchase the work, he stung them for 200,000 francs.

Monet's life at this time was full of difficulties, lack of money being the cause of much of them. Although he continued to paint over the next two years, his domestic conditions were unsettled and some paintings shown in a shop window which included *Women in the Garden*, which was ridiculed by the now jealous Manet, did not sell. He was now penniless and, leaving a now pregnant Camille, went to stay with his aunt. By the middle of 1868 he was dispossessed and penniless and had become so depressed that he is believed to have attempted suicide by drowning.

Mercifully, at this time, he managed to acquire his first patron, a M. Gaudibert, who had commissioned Monet to paint his wife (plate 12), and later in the year established him in a house in Fécamp, a seaside resort on the coast of Normandy.

Monet married Camille in 1870 just before the commencement of the Franco-Prussian War. After the outbreak, and to avoid involvement in the war, he left Camille alone with their three-year-old son and went to London. In the same year Paul Durand-Ruel, a young dealer, had staged an exhibition at the German Gallery in New Bond Street, London, the first exhibition of the Society of French Artists, in which Monet had one painting and from then until 1874 showed several times with the Society. During 1871 Monet was in England, Holland and Belgium whence he returned to Paris late in the year and in December rented a house at Argenteuil, then in a small town on the outskirts of Paris. In the following spring he was in Le Havre, in the summer Holland, and returned to Argenteuil in the autumn where he painted, with Renoir, a number of riverscapes on the Seine. For the subsequent five years, Monet's house became a favourite meeting place for most of the group and the many paintings done during this period, particularly those by Monet and Renoir, were the foundation of the Impressionist pictorial revolution. Indeed, it was in 1872 that Monet painted the work he

PLATE 8
Déjeuner sur l'herbe (1866)
Oil on canvas, 51$^{1}/_{8}$ x 71$^{1}/_{4}$ inches (130 x 181cm)

*This smaller version of the intended large composition for
Déjeuner indicates how Monet would have concentrated on the
sunlit pastoral scene. Camille was almost certainly the model for
the female figures and the composition in the previous plate can be
seen on the left-hand side while the figure of Bazille is repeated
in the figure on the right, stretched his full lanky length in the
foreground and wearing a hat in the centre background. It was
clearly an important work for Monet, his first great set-piece. He
was, however, discouraged by Courbet who saw the work in
progress and made unfavourable comments about it.*

PLATE 9

Women in the Garden (1866–67)

Oil on canvas 100$^{1/2}$ x 80$^{3/4}$ inches (255 x 205cm)

Monet's signature on this painting is an indication of the importance that he attached to it. It is a large painting and he submitted it to the Salon with the expectation that it would make his name known, and he made sure that it was not to be overlooked or misread. In the event, it was rejected by the Salon and for a time suffered indignities; firstly it was taken to Honfleur as Monet fled his creditors after slashing over 200 paintings to avoid their seizure; then, after the Salon rejection, it was exhibited in a dealer's shop window where it was ridiculed by Manet. In 1921 Monet eventually revenged himself for what he considered to be a slight by the Salon by charging the State, which was anxious

to obtain the picture, the extraordinary price of 200,000 francs. The painting was, Monet claimed, painted in the open-air 'on the spot after nature' in the garden of a house he had rented at Ville d'Avray. Camille was the model for all the figures and a trench was dug into which the large painting could be lowered to enable Monet to paint the upper part. For his friends this was a difficult and challenging work. It precedes the Impressionist method and shows something of the influence of Manet; but Monet's interest was in the effect of sunlight on the figures and foliage. Note the reflected light on the face of the girl in the foreground, thrown upwards from the white dress. Courbet commented that Monet had refused to paint the foliage in the background when the sun was not shining. The painting is composed in oppositions of light and dark, with spots of bright colour, and transforms Camille's hair into a strong brunette.

called *Impression: Sunrise*, a study of the docks at Le Havre (plate 20).

In 1873 another figure emerged who was to be influential in Monet's life, the well-heeled amateur painter and borderline Impressionist, Gustave Caillebotte, who became his patron and began to collect Impressionist work. His own works are not insignificant examples of the independent realism and in the broadest terms of inclusion could be termed an Impressionist.

The exhibition which established the group, introduced Impressionism and became the main outlet for their work until 1886, was held in 1874 at the former studio of the notable photographer Nadar, whose aim was to help the young and struggling painters. It was organized principally by Monet and Degas and was called the 'Première Exposition de la Société Anonyme des Artistes, Peintres, Sculpteurs, Graveurs' and opened on 15 April for one month. Monet exhibited five paintings and seven pastels.

MONET'S IMPRESSIONISM

The 1874 exhibition, now usually described as the first Impressionist exhibition, there being subsequent exhibitions (the last and eighth being held in 1886), is central to the early character of Impressionism. All the young independent painters exhibited but it was Monet who for the critics and public identified the character of

the movement as well as providing the name by which it has become known. Although they did not regard themselves as Impressionists at the time, most of them – to some extent all of them – contributed something to the perception of what constituted Impressionism. Degas did not like the name and his painting technique was very different from that of Monet. Renoir, who exhibited *La Loge*, one of his most famous works, in the first exhibition, came closer to Monet but every attempt at assessment of the qualities that are essentially Impressionist returns to Monet for justification. How closely does it actually identify with Monet?

It is important to remember that at the time of the first Impressionist exhibition, the painters were all young and their major works were still to be produced. This is particularly significant in the case of Monet whose last great waterlily paintings occupied him until his death in 1926. But it is true of all of them. The works that they showed in 1874 and earlier are those which established the name Impressionism but do not represent all the ramifications, digressions and experiments that each in their different ways, and variously influenced, incorporated in their later works.

If therefore we are to identify the revolution as that of the young painters it is to Monet, Pissarro, Sisley and Renoir that we turn. Manet never participated, Degas rejected the Impressionist name preferring independent or realist. It is Monet who offers the clearest ideas of early Impressionist work and particularly the stage at which he had arrived since settling in Argenteuil. It was here on the outskirts of Paris by the river Seine with his friends and colleagues, who in 1874 included Manet, that the best known and most closely linked Impressionist works were painted.

For Monet, water had always been a fascination, first on the seacoast near Le Havre and now on the river Seine. Capturing the movement of water, always a repetitious movement but never remaining the same, affected by light and weather, in different moods, had become for Monet, since his days with Boudin early in his development, a constantly demanding subject which, when painted in conjunction with moving foliage, demanded all his concentration. To capture the movement in an unchanging landscape was the basis of Impressionism for him. To seize what for Monet seemed the significant moment in any given potential subject was always his aim but which was inevitably frustrated by the time it took to

paint it. Each moment of significance demanded a different approach from its predecessor and perhaps many hours of painting time to realize it, during which time other significant moments intervened in a constant progression. It was necessary for time to stop which, of course, was not possible. Concentrated memory and a fluid technique, light and delicate dabs of colour where the forms lost definition which seemed almost to dissolve in light, were demanded on some occasions while on others the forms knit by tight paint application closely together gave a quickly completed image.

At this time, at Argenteuil, Renoir and the others were painting similar works in a similar technique and it is then that Impressionism speaks with its most unified voice. The immediacy of the transient moment engaged them all in their different ways, which could be considered a 'snapshot' approach but was not the case. Monet and the others did not forget or ignore the limits of the canvas or that they were constructing a picture within the long pictorial tradition of which composition was part of the

PLATE 10
The Terrace at Sainte-Adresse (1866)
opposite
Oil on canvas, 38½ x 51⅛ inches (98 x 130cm)

The view towards the Channel across the estuary of the Seine at Le Havre is taken from a window of Monet's aunt's villa and is a family portrait group. The seated figure is his father, a dignified and carefully modelled form; his aunt, Mme. Lecadre, is seated in the foreground under a parasol. The young couple in the background are Monet's cousin Jeanne-Marguérite and an unknown man. Although Monet is painting a scene with which he was familiar, as with Trains (plates 19, 28, 29), there is a message in the ships in the background. Old sailing ships, one a five-masted barque, and new steamships, their stacks belching smoke like trains, are consciously contrived to point up the change in sea travel and the importance of Le Havre as the chief port in France. Monet later observed that the flags placed on either side of the canvas were considered very daring at the time. The composition is a strange combination of closely drawn forms and loosely painted foliage. The water has a curiously patterned regularity of surface and tone which flattens the visual effect of the whole scene and draws attention to the distant ships and their message in a way that would not have been evident in actuality.

PLATE 11
The Beach at Sainte-Adresse (1867)
Oil on canvas, 22¼ x 32¼ inches (56 x 82cm)

As a child, Monet had played on this beach and in these boats and it remained one of his favourite haunts, full of happy memories. It was also the place where he painted with Boudin who must be counted as his first important influence and it was near here that he also met Jongkind, another source of inspiration. It is not surprising, therefore, that this work and other scenes of this area are not so much observation as an externalization of the pervasive presence in singularly calm and energetic images. In this painting, the scene is casually accurate and the drawing affectionately direct, the simple authority of the blue boat in the right foreground being the sign of a natural painter. There is a spatial, airy openness drawn into scale by the fishermen in the foreground, who are themselves simply painted – the one in black almost a caricature, a reminder of an early interest of Monet. The low horizon, reminiscent of the 17th-century Dutch landscapists, gives more than half the picture area to the sky, much more than is usual in Monet's later paintings, and is treated delicately to dominate and create the fresh open quality of his vision.

PLATE 12
Portrait of Madame Gaudibert (1868)
Oil on canvas, 85½ x 54⅓ inches (217 x 138cm)

This picture of Madame Gaudibert, the wife of Monet's first patron, Louis-Joachim Gaudibert, is the first of a number of significant portraits that Monet painted. It is treated as if it were a formal academic portrait, the figure dressed elegantly, and with the usual table and flowers in an interior of simple refinement. But the pose of the figure and the turn of the head gives it a sense of temporary, casual informality as if the subject is either unaware or uninterested in the fact that she is being painted, almost suggesting, perhaps, that Monet baulked at the formal requirements at the last moment. It shows how capable Monet was at achieving whatever he wished, having reached a level of technical accomplishment that enables one to infer that whatever he does is what he intends to do, uninhibited by inadequate technique. Louis-Joachim Gaudibert was a good friend to Monet. He was a collector and bought a number of Monet's paintings, enabling Monet and Camille with their newly-born son, Jean, to set up a home together in Etretât on the coast despite the fact that Monet, as usual, was soon to be penniless again.

training. What they were trying to avoid, however, was a continuation of the static posed images of classicism as still practised by the academicians. The inherent movement of life visible in all nature was part of their goal and this demanded both a new painting technique and new visual perceptions. Instead, therefore, of defining forms with line and colour they adopted a broken non-linear paint application which suggested or implied a visual flux. So far was this from academic practice, that their vibrant colour and interfusing of forms and voids with nervous, delicate or bold dashes of paint seemed to traditionalists to be mere incompetence. One critic, in 1877, commented of Monet and Cézanne: 'They provoke laughter and are altogether lamentable. They show the most profound ignorance of design, composition and colour. Children amusing themselves with paper and paints can do better.' This is an extreme but not unique type of criticism at this time, a case of unfamiliarity breeding contempt in this instance, and it is this new different treatment of familiar subjects that underlay the Impressionist revolution.

But there was more. Monet later in his life realized that the single image painted *en plein-air* was almost an impossibility if one was searching for the single, significant moment, because light constantly changes and the time taken to make one brushstroke detracts from the accuracy of the last and next. For him (and although it was a compromise he recognized and deplored), it became necessary to make a series of paintings of single subjects, such as the famous grain stacks, the poplar trees on the Epte, and the stream near Giverny. These works, which culminate in the great and ultimate long-lasting series of waterlilies are the culmination of Monet's personal and unique exploration of Impressionism.

AFTER ARGENTEUIL
Up to the time he left Argenteuil in 1877, Monet had already met most of the artists and supporters who had affected his career. In the previous year he had met the American-born John Singer Sargent who painted with him, the extraordinary collector Victor Chocquet whom he had met through Cézanne, and had visited the collector/financier Ernest Hoschedé at the Château de Montgeron. Hoschedé was a very wealthy man who, although he had already bought some of Monet's paintings, only knew him slightly. Also, in 1876, Monet had participated in the second Impressionist exhibition in the rue Le Peletier, showing 18 works. Remaining for the winter in Paris, he painted the well known *Gare Saint-Lazare* series (see example plate 29) in which a train engine features. Monet and the other Impressionists were devoted to nature and landscape subjects but it is interesting to note that the railway and trains appear frequently in their work. It seems that they were fascinated by the idea that the new

Continued on page 106

PLATE 13

Jeanne-Marguérite Lecadre in a Garden
(1866) below

Oil on canvas, 31½ x 39 inches (80 x 99cm)

In the mid 1860s Monet was experimenting with the various technical problems of translating natural effects effectively into paint, usually with a variety of brushes, sometimes with a palette knife or, as here, by using a brush to differentiate flat areas, such as the sky. These concerns become central to Monet's technique, leading in the 1870s to his essential Impressionism. Jeanne-Marguérite was Monet's cousin.

PLATE 14

The Luncheon (c. 1868–69) opposite

Oil on canvas, 75⅜ x 49¼ inches (191 x 125cm)

Monet's early life was punctuated by frequent crises, usually

financial, and he was fortunate that M. Gaudibert came to his aid in the summer of 1868 enabling the Monet family to rent a small house at Etretât, near Fécamp. It was a time of brief happiness. He told Bazille, who was godfather to his young son Jean: 'I am surrounded by everything I love.' Manet had already painted a luncheon scene which Monet probably had in mind since he had been a model for a preparatory sketch.

This is essentially a realist composition, carefully painted and with all the visual implications of the subject. Camille attends lovingly to Jean whose toys lie beneath the chair in the foreground, the maid is leaving, having set a typically French lunch and an unidentified visitor stands watching. And the viewer, outside looking in on this domestic scene, is involved by the steep perspective, carefully constructed to focus attention on mother and child. The place-setting in the foreground is obviously for Monet himself. A sense of immediacy is established by the objects awkwardly placed over the edge of the table, the newspaper, napkin and loaf of bread. A charming, if laboured pre-Impressionist work.

PLATE 15
La Grenouillère (1868) detail
Oil on canvas, 30 x 39³/₄ inches (77 x 101cm)

*The area along the Seine at Bougival and Croissy near Paris was
popular with young Parisian pleasure-seekers, literary figures and
the middle-rich, all of whom found something to entertain them;
swimming, eating, talking and drinking. The most popular resort
was La Grenouillère and its restaurant was owned by Père
Fournaise. For Monet and Renoir it was an attractive painting
location where they could sit side-by-side painting the same views.
Renoir's comments are interesting: 'The world knew how to laugh
in those days... I always stayed at Fournaise's. There were
plenty of girls to paint.' The hub of the radiating composition is
the circular 'camembert' and a catwalk joins it to the floating
pavilion on the right. Monet's work at this time is beginning to
approach the stabbing brushstrokes of Impressionism.*

PLATE 16
Hôtel des Roches-Noires, Trouville (1870)
opposite
Oil on canvas, 31¹/₂ x 21²/₃ inches (80 x 55cm)

*Monet was painting in Trouville with Boudin and this painting
shows Boudin's influence, particularly in the inclusion and
treatment of the figures. There is a delicacy and charming lightness
of touch in Monet's work, however, which is not evident in
Boudin. A small work, the scene is nevertheless full of a sense of
space, sunlight and an air of assurance and freedom typical of the
plein-air Impressionist approach. An observation by a visitor in
1874 describes the scene: 'The great building which seems to guard
the entrance to Trouville is the Hôtel des Roches-Noires. This is
the chief hotel, the resort of the most gaily dressed of the loungers;
it is worth seeing. There is not so much as a beggar to destroy the
illusion. Truly Trouville would have seemed a paradise to that
Eastern philosopher who wandered about in search of happiness;
and the paradise would last – perhaps till he was called on to pay
his hotel bill!'*

PLATE 17
Camille on the Beach, Trouville (1870)
above
Oil on canvas, 15 x 18¹/₈ inches (38 x 46cm)

*After a summer at Sainte-Adresse, in 1868 Monet painted a
number of subjects around Le Havre and only in the summer of
1870 did he go to Trouville with Camille and Jean. The influence
of Boudin is evident in this beach scene of the resort across the Seine
estuary from Le Havre, where the two painted together. Monet's
painting is much bolder than Boudin's and this small study could
almost be a detail of a larger work, so freely is the paint applied. It
was painted on the spot and grains of sand are embedded in the
pigment as evidence. The figure on the left is Camille, whom
Monet had married in June and she and Monet remained in
Trouville until September. Boudin, in a later letter, recalls the
occasion: 'I can still see you with that poor Camille at the Hôtel de
Tivoli … little Jean plays in the sand and his papa is seated on the
ground, a sketchbook in his hand – and does not work.' In
September Monet left Trouville and fled to London.*

PLATE 18

Madame Monet Wearing a Red Cape

(c. 1868–69)

Oil on canvas, 39¹/₃ x 31¹/₂ inches (100 x 80cm)

This sketch must have had a special significance for Monet which is unknown to anyone else. Is it an elaborated note of Camille's glance into the house as she passes, a momentary eye contact of great importance? We are entitled to speculate on this matter because it is the only early work that Monet kept with him for the rest of his life. It was probably painted in Etretât at the same time as The Luncheon (plate 14) in the winter of 1868–69 and is unfinished, broadly painted, and not designed to be an exhibition work. Nevertheless, it is an attractive work depending, necessarily, on the effect of immediacy that Monet succeeds in creating by the placing of Camille behind a grid of window panes in a relationship that is clearly not static although the broken up sharp red notes focus attention on the enigmatic expression of her face. Is it quizzical or sad?

Continued from page 99

technology, that was increasingly cutting swathes through open countryside or causing great iron and steel bridges to be built, was impressing a new modernity on nature. It is almost as if this was evidence of their appreciation of modern change.

During the whole of the later period at Argenteuil, Monet was desperately short of money. After a disastrous auction sale of Impressionist paintings in 1875, he was forced to ask Manet for a 20-franc loan and in 1877, after a second visit to the Hoschedés, again spent the winter in Paris soliciting or borrowing money from friends and patrons. In the following January he rented a house for his family at Vétheuil, on the Seine further from Paris. The year 1878 was especially dramatic – Camille was ill, Michel his second son was born, and the rent was not paid, which resulted in a crisis relieved again with the help of Manet. This was followed by a further complication. Hoschedé, the successful financier, had disguised from his partners and from his wife, Alice, the fact that his business affairs were in grave difficulties and when his associates called him to account, a disastrous situation was revealed. Despite deprivation of his directorships and the reduction of his shareholdings, he continued to live lavishly and, rather than attempt to explain the situation to his wife, fled to Belgium where he wrote desperate letters to her threatening suicide. She, with her six children had by this time joined the Monets at Vétheuil.

Camille's health steadily declined and she died in the following September. Monet, despite his genuine anguish at his wife's death, felt committed to showing works at the fourth Impressionist exhibition held that year in the Avenue de l'Opéra and submitted 29 paintings. After a disagreement with Degas, Monet, together with Renoir and Sisley, failed to show in the fifth Impressionist show and, in the case of Monet, also the sixth and, after a work was rejected in the Salon of 1880, did not submit again.

After Camille's death, further difficulties arose since Mme. Hoschedé was deeply religious and Monet was an atheist. She was exceedingly distressed at the irregularity of their household arrangements and, despite an increasing regard for one another, the couple could not marry since her husband was still alive. Monet was also deeply distressed at Camille's death. The result was an unhappy household and, in the hope of improving matters, they tried living in Pourville and Poissy, but unsuccessfully until, in 1883, Monet found a house at Giverny, a small village west of Paris on the Seine. For most of the year Monet travelled leaving his children with Alice while he painted on the Normandy coast, at Trouville, Fécamp, Dieppe, and Varengeville. In January 1883 he was painting at Le Havre and Etretât. At the end of April Manet died and Monet, after the funeral at which he was a pall-bearer, returned to Giverny.

PLATE 19
Train in the Country (1870)
Oil on canvas, 19²/₃ x 25¹/₂ inches (50 x 65cm)

*In the 19th century, the train was the ubiquitous symbol of
technology and progress, spreading across the countryside and
invading the life of the city. For the Impressionists, concerned as
they were with modern life, it was of particular interest and
importance and appears in many Impressionist paintings. This
characteristic landscape is divided horizontally by the speeding (in
the terms of those days) train, splitting the earth from the
heavens, smoke despoiling the sky.*

THE LAST PHASE

Monet lived at Giverny for the rest of his life (more than
40 years), visited by friends, fellow painters and, as his
fame increased, by national and international visitors. It
was the last great period of increasing security and
contentment, marred only by the eye trouble which by
the end of his life would leave him blind.

Giverny is a small village on the Seine near Vernon,
with hills on either side and two streams, the Ru and the
Epte in the valley, which divides the provinces of
Normandy and the Île de France. Monet's new house was
an unpretentious long, rather tall building, set in a garden
which, when Monet bought it, was typically bourgeois
and uninteresting. The ambience, nevertheless, was
attractive and the garden had great potential. Monet
immediately started to work on the property so that over
the years he was able to transform it into a famous and
exciting retreat, one which is now one of the most visited
properties with artistic connections. The village too, old–
fashioned with narrow streets, was delightful and the
surrounding landscape a constant attraction with poplars
lining the banks of the Epte and the fields well tended by
the simple peasants who viewed the Monets as curious,
strange and unwelcome additions to the village. Monet
was not well liked and his painting was regarded with
ignorant suspicion. The house and garden became a haven

PLATE 20
Impression: Sunrise (1872)
Oil on canvas, 18⁷⁄₈ x 24³⁄₄ inches (48 x 63cm)

This painting was unwittingly responsible for the naming of a movement in art that has enjoyed the most widely based popularity in the history of Western art – no mean trick. It is actually an attempt by Monet, in the context of his developing art, to make a small study of a sunrise in Le Havre, a transient moment he observed from a small boat in the harbour. The story of how it gave its name to Impressionism is told on page 86. The painting itself is an interesting, freely executed view into the rising sun, its reflection in the water being the only solidly painted element, with the docks and their machinery, the boats they serve, and the enveloping mist. It can be no more than the dictionary's definition of an impression – 'an immediate psychical effect of sensory stimulus'. With the work before our eyes, the sarcastic words of Louis Leroy, critic of Le Charivari *and responsible for attaching the word to the movement, will be of interest: 'What freedom, what ease of workmanship! Wallpaper in its embryonic state is more finished than THAT marine.'*

of seclusion for the increasingly reclusive painter and when Monet ventured out to paint grain stacks or poplars, local peasants threatened to destroy the stacks and cut the poplars down. The family's isolation was nevertheless a protection and Monet ran his household with military precision.

He needed money to accomplish his plans but it seems hardly necessary to mention that his shortage of money still continued. This condition prevailed for most of his long life, despite his increasing fame. Of course, his plans for Giverny were expansive and expensive, but Paul Durand-Ruel had been the main support of Monet and other Impressionists in the early years. Unfortunately, the year after Monet moved to Giverny, Durand-Ruel's bankers failed and he was unable to continue his support. Monet, in desperation, went to another dealer, Georges Petit, Durand-Ruel's rival in Paris and a rift opened between the two men because of this lack of loyalty. Although never fully healed, by 1890 Monet was again with Durand-Ruel on a better business footing but with a cooler personal relationship. He had just begun his series paintings, the first being of fields of poppies, poplars and grain stacks. At the same time he was continuing the transformation of the garden and at this time began the famous water garden which would contain the waterlilies he painted in a series of enormous panels, as well as in smaller studies. Spanning the water garden, he constructed

PLATE 21
Regatta at Argenteuil (c. 1872)
Oil on canvas, 18⅞ x 29½ inches (48 x 75cm)

Painted in broad slabs of colour in high key, this scene is illuminated by the brightest sunlight and exhibits a special joy and freshness, a visual delight, which reflects Monet's pleasure in the small town on the banks of the Seine. This painting, a small esquisse, or preliminary sketch, is built of broad directional form-constructing brushstrokes with great immediacy. The flat area patterning and the luminous colour reflect the influence of Japanese colour prints which, at that time, Monet was collecting. This is one of the works in the collection of Gustave Caillebotte, a rich collector and amateur painter who exhibited with and collected the work of Impressionist painters.

the Japanese bridge which he painted many times during the succeeding years and which, in sequential review, reveals the increasing deterioration of his sight.

His life at last was tranquil, his work was beginning to sell, he was getting semi-official recognition and was being visited by great figures of the day. In 1892, Monet began his impressive and much discussed series of Rouen Cathedral which eventually, it appears, amounted to about 30 paintings although the whereabouts of some is not now known. In 1888, and again in 1891, he visited London where he painted a number of scenes along the river Thames. These paintings carry echoes of Turner's work which Monet had seen in 1870 and admired. Turner's influence is evident in his work and the two had much in common. Later, however, Monet claimed that he did not much like Turner's work. Although the time Monet spent in London during the Franco-Prussian War is frequently said to have influenced him as a result of his seeing Turner's work, there is not as much direct evidence of this in his paintings as is often claimed. Perhaps more significant was the misty London river landscape he encountered after the clear sharp air and revealing light of France. There is, perhaps, more than a touch of Whistler's nocturnes in these paintings – Monet had originally met Whistler when they were students together at Gleyre's atelier and Whistler, a notable wit and fashionable exhibitionist, was becoming an increasingly important

PLATE 22
The Basin at Argenteuil (1872)
Oil on canvas, 23²/₃ x 31¹/₂ inches (60 x 80cm)

The bridge at Argenteuil, an important element in many Impressionist paintings during the period when Monet rented a house there, is seen here from the basin dock and forms a low horizon line, reminiscent of 17th-century Dutch paintings of a flat land. Within the land area, the horizontal banding of cast shadows on the left makes a strongly engaging pattern with the bridge and confirms the flatness of the whole land area. The sky, in contrast, is full of circular cloud forms swept by a brisk wind across the upper part from left to right. The difference between land and sky is central to the appreciation of the painting – a quiet land under a squally sky.

painter, as well as being one of the finest of etchers. There exists, however, one curious but interesting parallel between Turner and Monet. Both were passionately interested in the sea and its many moods. There is the well known story of Turner observing a storm at sea lashed to a mast. In 1893 Monet, accompanied by two friends, made a three-week trip on the liner *Normandie*. A tremendous storm blew up and while even the hardiest abandoned deck, Monet and his painter friend Blanche remained in securely fastened deck chairs to watch the storm's ferocity with similar Turnerian sangfroid.

Monet's presence in Giverny, as his fame grew, drew people of all kinds to the village. Many came, attracted by its charm, but the most dramatic effect was to transform the quiet rural locality into an artist colony. With no less than 40 studios being created in a village whose population had been only about 300, the change was dramatic and since that time Giverny has remained a place of pilgrimage for artists and art-lovers. Around this time Monet was well advanced in his plans for the garden, and was growing exotic trees and plants and designing walks and vistas.

There are many stories of his visitors. Clemenceau, an almost exact contemporary of Monet's, but who survived him by three years, became a close friend and admirer and a frequent visitor. Clemenceau, known as the 'Tiger of France', was twice prime minister and presided over the

PLATE 23
The Luncheon (c.1873)
Oil on canvas, 63 x 79¹/₈ inches (160 x 201cm)

After 1870, Monet did not submit his work to the Salon for a decade, but did exhibit in the first four Impressionist exhibitions, in the first showing not only Impression: Sunrise *(plate 20) but also seven pastels, three other medium-sized oils and a large oil,* The Luncheon, *which had been refused for the 1870 Salon. In the second 1876 Impressionist exhibition, he exhibited another painting referred to as a* panneau décoratif, *but subsequently also called* The Luncheon. *The earlier*

painting was an interior with Camille and Jean (plate 14), whereas the second depicts a table prepared for lunch and it is this one which is illustrated here. It is an isolated example not related to any preparatory sketches. It represents Camille and another figure moving towards the prepared table, with Jean playing nearby. There is a hat hanging from a tree with a strange black ribbon and a white rose lending a startling counterpoint to the approaching figures. This charming atmospheric work, originally described as a decorative panel, has been greatly admired by a number of painters and Bonnard produced a painting reminiscent of it.

PLATE 24
The Bridge at Argenteuil (1874)

Oil on canvas, $23\frac{3}{4}$ x $31\frac{1}{2}$ inches (60.5 x 80cm)

This is perhaps the archetypical Impressionist painting, completed in the year of the first Impressionist exhibition and depicting what can only be described as the early headquarters of the movement – Argenteuil and the Seine. It was here that the group met and painted together, sometimes side-by-side in front of the same subject. In the broken colour now characteristic, Monet has made as careful an observational study of the scene

as is possible, given the apparently casual nature of the subject. But this is deceptive: there is an ordered inevitability in the scene that is calculated and has resulted in a classical calm and balance. The boats are linked in a single solid unit and their masts with their reflections provide a stabilizing vertical. It is frequently supposed that Impressionist paintings, because they are concerned to give an 'impression', must be 'accidental' – that is to say, 'not composed'. One of the reasons why this work is representational is that it is so evidently composed. Absence of composition is not an identifying element in Impressionist work.

PLATE 25
A Corner of the Apartment (1875)
Oil on canvas, 32 x 23³/₄ inches (81.5 x 60.5cm)

In this strange but gripping painting, Monet has constructed a mysterious ambience into which to place his son Jean, who looks resigned as though accustomed to his role as a model. It is an affectionate study of a much-loved boy. He is placed on a highly patterned parquet floor and surrounded by outdoor plants, probably brought in for the winter, although it is a sunny day which means that the apartment is back-lighted. Monet had developed a habit of using blue in a particular way and he has used it in this painting to create the subdued lighting of the interior. Monet in fact listed the painting, when he sold it to Caillebotte in 1876, as Intérieur (tableau bleu).

Paris Peace Conference after the First World War. His influence and support were of great value to Monet. Cézanne visited in 1894 and met Clemenceau, Rodin and the critic and writer Geffroy. At the same time, the American painter Mary Cassatt was staying in the local hotel and met Cézanne during whose visit Renoir and Sisley came to dine and Cézanne, upset by their comments on his work which, though favourable, he misinterpreted as ridicule, left the house and all the paintings he had done during his stay, and he and Monet never met again. It was typical of Cézanne that he should leave his paintings behind and Monet, not believing – possibly incorrectly – that Cézanne would be much upset at their loss, sent them all on to him. Such anecdotes of the Monet ménage at Giverny abound.

After Ernest Hoschedé's death in 1891, any irregularities, as has been mentioned previously, were resolved by Monet's marriage to Alice in 1894. But the complications of Monet's family life did not end there when Jean, his elder son, married Alice's daughter Blanche in 1897 becoming both his step-daughter and daughter-in-law. Alice died on 19 May 1911 and Monet was devastated by her death, probably even more so than by Camille's as their life together had been longer and closer than his first marriage had been. All Monet's friends came to the funeral, even the near-blind Degas, and Monet seemed to lose interest in everything until autumn when

PLATE 26
La Japonaise (Madame Monet in Japanese costume) (1875–76)
Oil on canvas, 91¹/₈ x 56 inches (231.5 x 142cm)

Few lively and independent painters in France during the latter half of the 19th century failed to be engulfed by the waves of enthusiasm for all things Japanese which arose mainly from the import of coloured wood-block prints and subsequently from seeing the work of the great Japanese printmakers. Monet displayed this subtle influence in many of his landscapes from the early 1870s, but this painting is an extraordinary and unique homage to the Japanese style. The work is quite outside Monet's usual treatment of his subject, overtly contrived and painted in a style that he had long abandoned. Camille, looking more seductive and fey (her face in Renoir style) than in any other painting, is in a bizarre costume, probably based on a Japanese print. The robe would have been of silk but, as one critic noted, it looks more like homespun. The strongly painted samurai looks like a dwarf figure actually emerging into the scene. (Note the arms outside the line of the gown and the random disposition of the fans, jazzing the whole ensemble into a sort of visual frenzy.) A strange work but a great success – it sold for 2,000 francs. In 1918, when a friend told Monet that it had been resold for 150,000 francs, he replied that the purchaser had bought 'trash'. 'But yes, it was trash in being nothing but a caprice.' He also said the Camille was wearing a blond wig.

PLATE 27
Wild Poppies (1873)
Oil on canvas, 19²/₃ x 25¹/₂ inches (50 x 65cm)

In December 1871, after his return from England, Monet rented a house in Argenteuil which became the centre of the early stages of Impressionism. He was close to the river Seine and was able to pursue his study of the effects of water. The countryside around Argenteuil also interested him and provided another subject that he painted for a number of years – fields of red poppies – of which this is an early example. The next three years at Argenteuil was a relatively calm period for Monet and he made a number of tranquil, almost idyllic paintings often (as here) including Camille and Jean, now aged six. This one, in fact, includes Camille and her son twice, although Monet painted Jean differently attired. Camille is, however, wearing the hat that appears on the tree in plate 23. Although a casually structured work, the delicacy of touch, the fresh openness of the scene, the brilliant red of the poppies inviting the observer into the landscape, and the balancing firmness of the distant line of trees with the central dwelling to place humanity in nature, makes this a typically accomplished work from the maturing Monet.

he began to paint again. He discontinued his long painting trips, made almost every year, and became an almost total recluse, discouraging even his closest friends from visiting and rarely leaving his house and garden. He painted a number of Venetian scenes from memory and 29 of these were exhibited at the Bernheim Jeune Gallery in Paris in 1912. Monet was disappointed with his work at this time but, more seriously and like Degas, realized his eyesight was failing and was eventually diagnosed as having a double cataract for which he refused an operation, fearful of losing his vision altogether.

In February 1914, before the outbreak of the First World War, Jean Monet died and Blanche, his widow, became Monet's companion and housekeeper for the rest of his life. During the first two years of the war, within sight and sound of guns and troop movements he was immured at Giverny, depressed and without the will to paint. During this period Clemenceau, even though involved in affairs of state and, later in the war, was prime

PLATE 28
Train in the Snow (1875)
Oil on canvas, 23¼ x 30¾ inches (59 x 78cm)

Two aspects of Monet's subject interests are combined in this painting. He was interested in unusual weather effects, particularly winter snow and ice, and painted many landscape studies of the colour differences between winter and summer light effects. He was also interested in the railway and the new systems that were spreading across France. His house in Argenteuil was near the railway and the track ran through his property at Giverny without, it appears, any disturbance to him. This painting is a remarkably effective treatment of an overcast winter day in close tones of grey and shades of yellow ochre, with the sharp orange headlights surrounded by a dull warm red giving the train a welcoming appearance in a chill landscape.

PLATE 29
The Gare Saint-Lazare, Paris (1877)
Oil on canvas, 29³/₄ x 41 inches (75.5 x 104cm)

The importance of the railways to the Impressionists has already been noted and this is an important and effective demonstration of Monet's ability to find a pictorial method of translating this innovation, dominated by steam and smoke, iron and glass, with the new mechanical monsters at the fulcrum. Monet produced other versions of the subject in his last major series as commentaries on modern society. The viewpoint is one which passengers would have been familiar with, the station's terminal looking towards the Pont de L'Europe which forms a hazy rectangular block emphasized at each end by smoke or steam in sunlight. The engine is belching a delicate mauve smoke which rises to the containing broad triangle of the shed roof. To the left of the engine is a carriage while on the right, in sunlight, the waiting passengers stand motionless while sunlight pouring through the glass panels of the roof intensifies the effect of steam and smoke which swirls around them. The central line of the painting is the pitch of the roof and taken together, the whole evokes an 'impression' of the gothic nave of a cathedral which, when one recalls Monet's atheism, makes a fitting setting for the modern, secular 'religion' of industry and commerce.

PLATE 30

The Rue Montorgueil: Fête of 30 June 1878

Oil on canvas, 31¹/₂ x 20 inches (80 x 50.5cm)

Monet's last paintings of a Paris subject are the two (the other is the smaller Rue Montorgueil Decked Out with Flags) *he made at the national fête of 30 June in the year of the Exposition Universelle, the first since the Franco-Prussian War and the Commune. The scene in the rue Montorgueil is an exciting interplay of diagonals, vertical strokes and complicated*

criss-crossing of the national colours in the flags, painted with verve and enthusiasm. It is surely intended as an impression in the true sense of the word. Recalling the scene much later, Monet reminisced, 'I like flags very much. At the first Fête Nationale, of June 30th, I was walking along rue Montorgueil with my painting equipment. The street was decked with flags, but swarming with people. I spied a balcony, mounted the stairs and asked permission to paint. It was granted... Ah, those were good times, though life was not always easy ... '

minister, spent time and much trouble trying to encourage Monet to paint. He suggested that Monet undertake some large water paintings, stimulating his enthusiasm so much that he had a large studio built, 75ft long and 49ft high (23 and 15 metres) which he stacked with large canvases. This gave Monet new heart to the extent that he began to work assiduously on paintings, sketches and studies related to what became an extensive project, known as the *Décoration des Nymphéas*, which he intended to present to the State. Without Clemenceau and Blanche, this work would never have been completed. Monet was tempted to abandon it as his eyesight worsened and he overpainted work already done, almost ruining it in the process. Clemenceau once threatened that he would never speak to Monet again if he broke his promise and failed to finish the programme. Supported by Blanche who encouraged Monet every day, Clemenceau persuaded Monet to continue what was in itself a daunting task for a man nearly blind and almost beyond his powers. Nevertheless, the *Nymphéas* were eventually finished and after some discussion were located in the Orangerie of the Tuileries in 1927.

Like Degas, Monet continued to work when almost blind until, by October 1926, he was in considerable pain and his doctors diagnosed pulmonary sclerosis. He died on 5 December 1926 in his much-loved home at Giverny. He was given a quiet funeral without religious ceremony

which, as a non-believer, was his wish. The pallbearers at his funeral were Clemenceau, and the painters Bonnard, Roussel and Vuillard. There was not even a funeral oration, only flowers. 'I perhaps owe having become a painter to flowers,' he said in 1924.

THE LAST WORKS

The final decade of Monet's life was overshadowed by his steady loss of sight, despite eventually accepting an operation for cataract in 1923, which partially restored the sight in one eye. The studies he made of parts of his garden or lily pond are poignant evidence of his growing inability to control either line or colour. He did a number of views of the Japanese bridge, for instance, in which the bridge itself is, as a form, hardly discernible. These last paintings are canvases without form but reveal the potent impact of a painter for whom colour without form was not only almost the only discernible result of applying paint but also was, as it had always been, his abiding interest. For him, from the early tentative beginnings, the small searching dabs and short strokes of colour which suggested both form and moving nature had remained a constant inspiration. In the last works, apart from the *Nymphéas*, the colour is intense and unrefined as his vision only allowed him to see the strongest colours.

There was considerable fear that he would destroy the effect of the large *Nymphéas* panels that had already been

PLATE 31

Snow Effect at Vétheuil: Looking Towards the Church (1878–79)

Oil on canvas, 20½ x 28 inches (52 x 71cm)

Early in 1878 Monet left Argenteuil (and Paris) for Vétheuil where he began a period of hard work during which (although they are not given the attention of the earlier works from the Argenteuil period) he produced a number of fine calm paintings of the town and its surroundings. Vétheuil is on the Seine and Monet lived not far from the water he so much loved, near an eminently paintable section of the river with its small island and rich vegetation and tall poplars along its banks. The snow scene here must have been painted from one of the small islands or from Monet's bateau atelier or floating studio. The whole ambience of the picture and the colour key is a remarkably evocative image of the chill of the snow-enveloped town.

worked on and it took all of Clemenceau's persuasion and authority to prevent this happening. Thus the latter period of Monet's working life was a collaboration, albeit confrontational, between the great prime minister of France, the 'Tiger', Monet's closest friend and supporter, and the near-blind painter who desperately wanted to improve, as was always his endeavour, the last great paintings of the late Impressionists, the *Nymphéas* (plates 47–49). We must be grateful that both triumphed in the end. But it was a late ending to the most significantly influential development of 19th-century painting. All the great movements of early 20th-century art had commenced – and most finished – before Monet died, a legendary and venerated figure but, as it seemed then, an artistic irrelevance. Later, and wiser one hopes, we now see Monet as one of the great revolutionaries of modern painting and a founding father of 20th-century style.

PLATE 32
Bordighera (1884)
Oil on canvas, 25½ x 31⅞ inches (65 x 81cm)

Monet arrived in Bordighera in January 1884. The seaside town is just beyond the French Riviera, over the border in Italy, and Monet was so enchanted with the place that although he had intended to stay for only a month, in fact he remained in the area until April, painting with great diligence and enthusiasm. He covered dozens of canvases – five or six a day (according to his frequent letters to Alice) and also managed to write, constantly assuring Alice that he would return in a few days. Soon after he arrived he tried to describe to her the alarming brilliance of the colour that surrounded him: 'I am appalled at the colours I am having to use … and yet I am really understating it.' It was a liberating time for him, nonetheless, as it obliged him to heighten the tone of his pictures, thicken the paint and widen his colour range.

PLATE 33
The Rocks at Belle-Île: La Côte Sauvage
(1886)

Oil on canvas, 25½ x 32 inches (65 x 81.5cm)

*The isolated Belle-Île, off the Quiberon peninsula of Brittany
and facing the Bay of Biscay, was Monet's painting ground in
late 1886. The cliffs and rocks off the Côte Sauvage, exposed to
the wild Atlantic weather, seems a strange location for Monet to
have discovered, but he thoroughly explored the rugged coast and
a series of dramatic evocations resulted. He described it as a ' ...
terrible, sinister country, but very beautiful ... the ocean is so
beautiful that I have begun a quantity of studies ... but such
terrible weather. I work in the rain and wind.' The treatment is
similar to that used by Monet when he arrived on the
Mediterranean coast (plate 32) but the elements are in a very*

*different mood. The precise subject of this work are the needles of
Port-Coton, the most awe-inspiring of the extraordinary
weathered formations of this rocky island. An interesting anecdote
related by Gustave Geffroy, Monet's future biographer and friend
who was art critic on Clemenceau's newspaper* La Justice
*concerns Monet's visit. Geffroy came to Belle-Île for a holiday in
October and was sitting at a table at his inn when he discovered
that he was on a table reserved for a painter who soon came in, 'a
rough man, tanned, bearded, wearing heavy boots, dressed in
coarse material, a sailor's beret on his head, a wooden pipe
projecting from his rough beard, and in the centre of all that, a
fine profile and an intelligent eye'. Geffroy had already given
favourable reviews of Monet's work though he had never met
him; they met, ate together, drank and remained the closest of
friends for life.*

PLATE 34
London: The Houses of Parliament (1904)
Oil on canvas, 31⁷/₈ x 36¹/₄ inches (81 x 92cm)

From late in 1899 until the spring of 1904, Monet worked on paintings of London, initially from his room in the Savoy Hotel, overlooking the Thames and with a view of the Houses of Parliament not far away to the right. He chose this subject and the area surrounding it for a series that he worked on over a number of visits lasting four years, hoping that he would be able to arrange an exhibition of his work in London. Although this did not materialize, Monet did show 37 of the series at Durand-Ruel's gallery in Paris throughout May 1904. Between his visits to London he worked at Giverny on his waterlily paintings, painted at Vétheuil and took an automobile trip with Alice, to Madrid, to see Velásquez's paintings in the Prado. He also worked at Giverny on his London (Thames) series, working from memory during 1905 and still hoping to exhibit in London.

The example illustrated here, and subtitled 'A Hole in the

Mist Made by the Sun', indicates the range of Monet's interest in this single subject. Not only is the approach different from other versions but the technique is also varied according to his appreciation of the conditions. The treatment of the misty evening scene is more reminiscent of Turner than any other, in the indistinctly emerging forms. It is important to remember, as previously mentioned, that Monet worked on these after he returned home, obviously confident of his retentive memory and powers of recall and, even more interestingly, confirming the plein-air obsession he is supposed to have had. Much later he expressed his view of London and the Thames: 'I loved London so much, but ... only in winter... It is a mass, an ensemble, and it is so simple. But above all in London I love the fog... It is the fog that gives it its magnificent amplitude; its regular and massive blocks become grandiose in that mysterious mantle... How could English painters ... have painted the houses brick by brick? These people painted bricks that they did not see, could not see!'

PLATE 35
Cliffs at Etretât: The Manneport, Reflections in the Water (1885)
Oil on canvas, 26 x 32 inches (66 x 81.5cm)

By August 1884, after leaving Bordighera, Monet was back in Etretât where he painted more studies of the dramatic cliffs and tumultuous seas which he had begun in 1883 and continued, with interruptions, until late in 1885. During this time he gave his attention to studies of the sea and cliffs in all weathers, making use of a variety of treatments. In this example, painted broadly and loosely, he effectively captures the play of reflections on moving water.

PLATE 36
Woman with a Parasol, turning to the right
(1886)
Oil on canvas, 51½ x 34⅔ inches (131 x 88cm)

During the late 1880s, Monet decided to abandon landscapes and make some figure studies. A number of stories surround this decision, one of the more interesting (told in different versions and improved upon, no doubt) concerns Monet's wish to hire a model to pose for a beach scene with nude bathers. Alice, her sensibilities affronted, is reported as declaring that the day the model came was the day she would leave. This is taken to explain the fact that, although Monet did make a number of figure paintings, they are all clothed and the models used were almost invariably from members of his large, close family. As early as 1875–78 Monet had made a painting of a woman with a parasol in an almost identical pose as the one illustrated, but turning to the left and including a small boy, which identified it as Camille and Jean. The painting is very much a sketch, while the later version, omitting the child, is in the style that Monet had developed by the 1880s.

PLATE 37
Boating at Giverny (c. 1887)
Oil on canvas, 38½ x 51½ inches (98 x 131cm)

Among the figure studies Monet painted in the late 1880s, it is not surprising to find a number connected with water and boating. This affectionately perceived family group is pictured on a quiet backwater of the river Epte and the work is a closely woven tapestry of dark greens and blues against which the boat and the figures with their reflections are a tranquil evocation of a fashionable Sunday outing, the effects of sunlight being subtly indicated only on the dresses of the young figures who are casually fishing. The girls are probably three of Monet's stepdaughters. The unusual compositions of these boating paintings are an indication of Monet's strong individualism: 'I so want to prove that I can do something different.'

PLATE 38

Grain Stacks: At the End of the Summer, in the Morning (1891) previous pages

Oil on canvas, 23²/₃ x 39¹/₃ inches (60 x 100cm)

The choice of grain stacks, a seemingly unpromising subject for a series of paintings arose, it is said, from a walk Monet took with his step-daughter, Blanche, along high ground near his house when he saw a distant grain stack shining almost white in the sun and decided to paint it. He rushed home for his paints only to find that the stack had, as might be expected, changed in colour and aspect. The solution was for Alice to supply him with a succession of canvases so that he could start another as soon as the light changed. The result was a series which reflected all the changes which had occurred to the stacks over a given span of time; this gave him sufficient information to enable him to undertake further work on the subject in his studio. The number contained in the series is not clear but he sold the 15 exhibited in the three days of his show at Durand-Ruel's in 1891 at prices ranging from 3–4,000 francs. It is interesting to note, in this example, that the more distant stack is in a lower key than the nearer and with a greater tonal range, a reversal of the usual. It is the smaller scale that places the one that is more distant.

PLATE 39

Rouen Cathedral (1894) above

Oil on canvas, 39³/₄ x 25¹/₂ inches (101 x 65cm)

Monet's highly renowned series of paintings of the façade of Rouen Cathedral numbered over 30 paintings (the exact number is not certain) and depicts the west front from slightly different viewpoints at various times of the day from dawn to dusk. The series was begun from the second-floor window of a shop opposite the façade in the winter of 1892 and through 1893 and was later completed at Giverny. Monet's 1895 show at Durand-Ruel's gallery included 20 cathedrals out of the total of 50 paintings exhibited. Eighteen of these were of the façade of the cathedral. In his newspaper, La Justice, Clemenceau praised these works which he entitled 'The Revolution of Cathedrals', and which he separated into four groups; grey, white, iridescent and blue. Perhaps the first important point to be made is that they are paintings of a flat façade, unchanged and unchanging, with little indication of volume or, as George Moore perceptively observed, '... views of the cathedral without once having recourse to the illusion of distance. Form is discernible but, and here the essential element, the influence of the series is to be identified; it is on the surface of the painting and has to be constructed spatially by the viewer; it is the nearest to the abstraction of the real that the 19th century offers.' Moore went on to suggest that Monet had 'striven by thickness of paint and roughness of handling to reproduce the very material quality of the stonework'. The tactility of the surface itself, creating and denying the identity of the cathedral, is another part of the inspiration of these astonishing constructions. It is also important to remember that although they were started on the spot, they were completed in the studio at Giverny where the painting assumed its own internal reality.

PLATE 40

Rouen Cathedral (1894) opposite

Oil on canvas, 42¹/₈ x 29¹/₂ inches (107 x 75cm)

PLATE 41
Cliff at Varangeville: The Gorge of Petit-Ailly (1897) detail
Oil on canvas, 25½ x 36¼ inches (65 x 92cm)

Because of the absence of snow in Giverny, Monet once more spent the winters of 1896 and 1897 on the northern coast, at Varengeville, Pourville and Dieppe. He confessed that it was a joy for him to see the movement of the sea again. But this was not Normandy's only attraction as far as Monet the gourmet and painter was concerned. The landscape was among the most varied in France with its golden beaches and sea-sculpted cliffs. Its cuisine was distinctive, based on cheese, butter, cream, fish, fine chickens, cider and liqueurs. But despite all this, it was still the sea and the chalk cliffs that above all fascinated Monet and
inspired some of his most potent images in a number of short series. Of the paintings made on these visits, the one of the gorge at Varengeville is the most dramatic. The small house, which Monet painted separately in a number of studies (14 times in 1897), is the local customs house and dates from the time of Napoleon when it was built as a post for French customs officials on the lookout for contraband. Since the fall of Napoleon it had been appropriated by local fishermen. Its presence in these paintings, apart from offering a focal interest, seems to suggest the struggle of man in the face of relentless nature on land and sea. The way Monet painted it varied from an expression of poignant isolation to self-contained heroism and even, as in this example, to its portrayal as an idyllic tourist haven with passing pleasure boats.

PLATE 41 ——— 140 ———

PLATE 42
Poplars on the Epte (1891)
Oil on canvas, 39 x 25$\frac{1}{5}$ inches (100 x 65cm)

During the 1890s, Monet turned to series painting, due partly to the problem that confronts all plein-air painters; the inability to capture the subject before it changes its physical appearance. Light and its effects all change by the minute, as does the restless movement of vegetation, sea and sky. Monet's three best known series are Grain stacks (Haystacks), plate 38, Rouen Cathedral (plates 39 and 40), and Poplars. Since, Monet could paint a number of versions in a day, the series paintings offer a unique opportunity to study the range and motivation of his treatment of a single subject but presents a problem when considering the series

within the limitations of a book. This must stand as representative of over 20 different versions of this row of poplars on the banks of the Epte near Giverny. Monet feared that they were about to be cut down but, with reckless but characteristic originality, solved the problem by coming to a financial arrangement that they would not be destroyed until he had finished painting them. His choice of this subject is another element in his search for something different. A long winding row of verticals, each subtly different but basically the same, each a living and unique object and a simple rigid geometrical element, are linked horizontally to both land and water, changing in the open sunlight and presenting a daunting but fascinating problem. The effectiveness of these dignified verticals is a measure of Monet's success.

PLATE 43
The Japanese Bridge at Giverny (1899)
detail
Oil on canvas, 35 x 36²/₃ inches (89 x 93cm)

For most of his life Monet had been beset by money troubles but, by the 1890s, he had achieved such wealth that he was able to lavish money on Giverny, turning it into a horticultural wonderland and indulging his imaginative fancies. The result was a unique property, developed by a peasant genius with rare talents. Among the great projects Monet created was the famous waterlily pool and Japanese bridge, which he painted many times in his last days when he was almost a recluse, confined to his much loved estate. Monet managed to get planning permission in 1893 and worked on the design, altering it over many years until 1910. Initially, and surprisingly, he did not make many paintings of the lily pond – only three in the period up to 1897. Thereafter, he made a number until the early 1920s when his eyesight had so deteriorated that it was almost impossible for him to discern forms. The painting here, dating from 1899, is a calm evocation of this delightful spot, executed in the familiar short-stroke technique of his mature years.

The detail in this plate indicates much about Monet's technique and his failing eyesight. While the small touches of paint are not as surely placed as in his earlier work, the delicacy of his colour perception and the textural differentiation of form is still evident. Monet has confessed to Geffroy earlier, ' I planted my waterlilies for fun, when I saw, all of a sudden, that my pond had become enchanted. I seized my palette. Since then I have had no other model.' The lily pond, of which the Japanese bridge was the focal point, became the inspiration for the late great Nymphéas panels and paintings.

PLATE 44
Pond of the Nymphéas (1904)
Oil on canvas, 35$^1/_2$ x 36$^1/_4$ inches (90 x 92cm)

After buying a strip of land in 1890, Monet set about transforming it into a shallow pond and diverting water from the Epte to fill it. A variety of waterlilies were placed in it and around the edges bamboo and weeping willows were planted. Over it, he constructed a Japanese bridge and made his first painting of the finished effect in 1892. From this time to the end of his life the pond remained an important, one might almost say central, interest in his life and was the inspiration for the last great Nymphéas murals. As mentioned above, Monet spent much time after 1900 in Giverny painting his garden

and the famous lily pond with its Japanese bridge. Here again, Monet is influenced in his technical treatment by the conditions which confront him. This painting suggests the fascination of a new discovery that Monet was exploring at this time. The flat, still surface of the pond and the clarity of the reflected lily plants on that surface, almost equal in visual intensity to actual plants, both break up the sense of the water surface and give him new compositional opportunities with the square format which attracted him. The result is a series of paintings which explore, in a way different from Cézanne's concern with the same problem, the presentation of a flat pictorial space which at the same time emphasizes the painting's physical identity as a flat surface, while creating a sense of the subject's different spatial identity.

PLATE 45
The Grand Canal, Venice (c. 1908) above
PLATE 46
Gondolas in Venice (c. 1908) left
(Both pastel on paper/oil sketch)

In 1908 Monet, depressed, in poor health and unhappy with his work, was invited to visit American friends of the painter John Singer Sargent in Venice. Although unenthusiastic and unimpressed by the romantic Venetian myth he was immediately entranced by the 'unique light'. As he wrote to Gustave Geffroy: 'It is so beautiful. I console myself with the thought of returning next year ...But how unfortunate not to have come here when I was younger, when I was full of audacity.'

The two sketches are in pastel, a medium occasionally used by Monet (in earlier years he had an exhibition of pastels) and it is surprising that he did not make more use of the method that made Degas such a unique practitioner and might have seemed a method highly appropriate for Impressionist treatment. The delicate light effects here are akin to the London series of a few years earlier.

PLATES 47
Nymphéas top

PLATES 49
Nymphéas bottom

The scope and scale of these enormous and creative panels were a constant reminder to the knowledgeable art aficionados of the French art establishment of Monet's role in the new art that was being created by the young artists of the modern movements of this century; such figures as Picasso, Matisse and Braque. It is impossible in a book to do more than indicate the scale and awesome grandeur of these panels. Details may be shown but the best indications of the nature of these works is perhaps offered by the photograph of Monet himself among them, remembering that at this time he could barely see the small sections upon which he was working and never the whole sweep of the compositions. The truth is that only a visit to the Orangerie in Paris will provide the possiblity of a real experience of Nymphéas.

PLATE 48
Monet in his specially built studio at Giverny working on the Nymphéas panels
centre

PLATE 50
The Japanese Bridge, Giverny (1918)
Oil on canvas, 39$^{1}/_{3}$ x 78$^{3}/_{4}$ inches (100 x 200cm)

As the years passed after his temporary loss of sight in one eye as the result of an accident in 1901, Monet suffered increasingly from *eye trouble resulting in acute depression only relieved by his visit to Venice in 1908. But after the death of Alice in 1911, he hardly left Giverny and was cared for by Blanche, Jean's widow, who supported and encouraged him. By this time his vision was very poor and his hand none too steady so that the agitated surfaces of many of his later paintings is not the development of a new*

method but more of a determination to continue his painting at all cost. This view of the Japanese bridge still evokes the structure of the scene but lacks the controlled direction which his earlier work always contained. At this time Monet increasingly suffered fits of despondency during which he roused himself to an almost feverish pitch of activity which expressed itself in bold uncontrolled colour and brushstrokes. The passionate intensity of these works is exceedingly moving.

ACKNOWLEDGEMENT

The Publishers wish to thank the following for providing photographs, and for permission to reproduce copyright material. While every effort has been made to trace and acknowledge copyright-holders, we wish to apologize should any omissions have been made.

Woman from Normandy in Profile
Musée Marmottan/Giraudon, Paris

Young Dandy with Monocle and Cigar
Musée Marmottan/Giraudon, Paris

Photograph of Monet
Musée Marmottan/Giraudon, Paris

Trophies of the Hunt
Musée d'Orsay/Giraudon, Paris

Édouard Manet's Déjeuner sur l'herbe
Musée d'Orsay/Giraudon, Paris

Still-Life: The Joint of Beef
Musée d'Orsay/Giraudon, Paris

The Walkers (Study for Déjeuner sur l'herbe)
Washington National Gallery of Art/Giraudon, Paris/Lauros

Déjeuner sur l'herbe
Pushkin Museum, Moscow/Giraudon, Paris

Women in the Garden
Musée d'Orsay/Giraudon, Paris

The Terrace at Saint-Adresse
The Metropolitan Museum of Art, New York/ Giraudon, Paris/ Lauros

The Beach at Saint-Adresse
Art Institute, Chicago/Giraudon, Paris

Portrait of Madame Gaudibert
Louvre, Paris/Lauros/Giraudon, Paris

Jeanne-Marguérite Lecadre in a Garden
Hermitage Museum, St Petersburg/Giraudon, Paris

The Luncheon (1868–69)
Stadelsches Kunstinstitut, Frankfurt/Giraudon, Paris

La Grenouillère
Metropolitan Museum of Art, New York. Bequest of Mrs H. O. Havemeyer, 1929. The Havemeyer Collection/Giraudon, Paris

Hôtel des Roches-Noires, Trouville
Musée d'Orsay/Giraudon, Paris/Lauros

Camille on the Beach, Trouville
Musée Marmottan/Giraudon, Paris

Madame Monet Wearing a Red Cape
Cleveland Museum of Art/Lauros/Giraudon, Paris

Train in the Country
Musée d'Orsay/Lauros/Giraudon, Paris

Impression: Sunrise
Musée Marmottan/Giraudon, Paris

Regatta at Argenteuil
Musée d'Orsay/Lauros/Giraudon, Paris/Knudsens

The Basin at Argenteuil
Musée d'Orsay/Giraudon, Paris

The Luncheon (c. 1873)
Musée d'Orsay/Lauros/Giraudon, Paris

The Bridge at Argenteuil
Musée d'Orsay/Giraudon, Paris

A Corner of the Apartment
Musée d'Orsay/Lauros/Giraudon, Paris

La Japonaise

(Mme. Monet in Japanese costume)
Boston Museum of Fine Arts/Lauros/Giraudon, Paris

Wild Poppies
Musée d'Orsay/Giraudon, Paris

Train in the Snow
Musée Marmottan/Giraudon, Paris

The Gare Saint-Lazare
Musée d'Orsay/Giraudon, Paris

The Rue Montorgueil: Fête of 30 June 1878
Musée d'Orsay, Paris

Snow Effect at Vétheuil
Musée d'Orsay/Giraudon, Paris

Bordighera
Chicago Fine Art Institute/Lauros/Giraudon, Paris

The Rocks at Belle-Île: La Côte Sauvage
Pushkin Museum, Moscow/Giraudon, Paris

London: The Houses of Parliament
Musée d'Orsay/Giraudon, Paris

Cliffs at Etretât:

The Manneport, Reflections in the Water
Musée d'Orsay/Giraudon, Paris

Woman with a Parasol, turning to the right
Musée d'Orsay/Giraudon, Paris

Boating at Giverny
Musée d'Orsay/Giraudon, Paris

Grain Stacks:

At the End of the Summer, in the Morning
Musée d'Orsay/Lauros/Giraudon, Paris

Rouen Cathedral
Musée d'Orsay/Giraudon, Paris

Rouen Cathedral: The Façade
Louvre/Lauros/Giraudon, Paris

Cliff at Varengeville: The Gorge of Petit-Ailly
Musée des Beaux-Arts Andre Malraux, Le Havre/Giraudon, Paris

Poplars on the Epte
National Gallery of Scotland

The Japanese Bridge at Giverny
Musée d'Orsay/Giraudon, Paris

Pond of the Nymphéas
Musée des Beaux-Arts, Caen/Giraudon, Paris

The Grand Canal, Venice
Ancienne Collection Brame et Lorenceau/Giraudon, Paris

Gondolas in Venice
Musée des Beaux-Arts, Nantes/Giraudon, Paris

Nymphéas
Musée de l'Orangerie/Lauros/Giraudon, Paris
Musée d'Orsay/Lauros/Giraudon, Paris

Monet in his studio working on the Nymphéas panels
Musée Marmottan/Giraudon, Paris

Nymphéas
Musée de l'Orangerie/Lauros/Giraudon, Paris

The Japanese Bridge, Giverny
Musée Marmottan/Giraudon, Paris

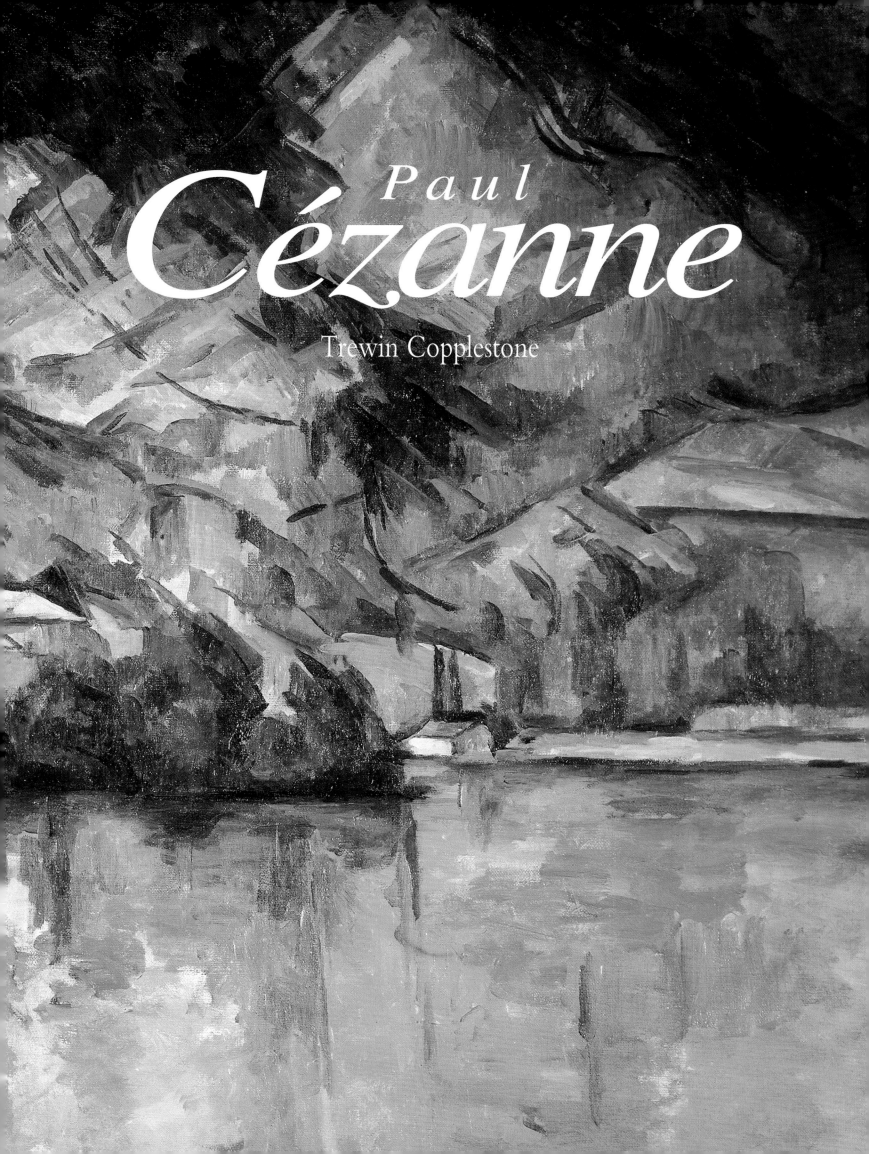

Paul
Cézanne

Trewin Copplestone

PLATE 1
Paul Cézanne (1839-1906)

At times, when one reads art critics or historians of 20th-century art, it may seem that the whole structure rests on a foundation called Cézanne. The first movements of the century, Fauvism and Cubism, were led respectively by Matisse and Picasso, and both, despite very different approaches to painting, claimed Paul Cézanne as their mentor and source of inspiration. It is certain that the qualities discerned in Cézanne's work by almost all writers have been seminal to many of the varied directions that painting has taken in the last 100 years, not only in Europe but worldwide as art has become an international enterprise. That Cézanne is the epic icon from which so much of 20th-century art derives its faith and inspiration is somewhat surprising when one examines his decidedly unheroic life in term of positive action or open revolution. Cézanne was never a leader as were many of the French painters – Ingres, Delacroix, Manet or Monet in his own day, Picasso, Matisse or Mondrian in this century. And yet his pre-eminence is hardly disputed and his influence persists.

One may go further and say that Cézanne's reputation is all the more surprising when one recognizes that his art is both difficult and not as immediately attractive to the observer as, for instance, the works of Monet or Degas; neither do they offer the challenge and drama of a Van Gogh or a Gauguin. To add yet one more element of difficulty: he is what is often described as a 'painter's

painter'. In other words, it is considered that many, if not most, of his painterly qualities can only be initially appreciated by fellow professionals; for the ordinary picture-lover there often remains the underlying uncertainty of the real value of his work. It is certainly true that he did not have the fluency of drawing or the easily absorbed subject-matter of his contemporaries. Since his death there has been a great deal of eulogistic writing, but there has also been caution and, in a few cases, dismissal. And then one looks at the sale values and asks oneself what there is in these works that explains the prices they command.

Altogether then, a great but difficult painter, whose work, it appears, must be explained before it can be appreciated and enjoyed, and even then one wonders if enjoyment is the right word to identify the experience. It should be said that painting is a language of the eye that appeals to both the visual sense as well as the mind. It is not literature nor is it photography. It has often been said that if a picture could be entirely translated into words, leaving nothing to be communicated, it would not have used its own visual language to make an essential statement.

It is consequently important to attempt to identify what Cézanne's achievement actually was. This is not easy. At a conference concerned with art education at the Institute of Contemporary Art in London some years ago,

PLATE 2

Still–Life with Leg of Mutton and Bread

(1865–67)

Oil on canvas, 10²/₃ x 13³/₄ inches (27 x 35cm)

Cézanne's technique in the early work is well illustrated in this painting. He uses a heavy impasto, applied with both brush and (more often) a palette knife, which almost suggests a modelled form in bas relief. As can be seen in the leg of mutton, he used

the knife to follow round the form or (with the lower leg) along it to suggest its structure and feeling. It is clearly the work of someone who is discovering the problems of representational painting. The loaf of bread is an almost amorphous mass and the whole work is constructed in a traditional tonal form. It is because it is so far from the recognizable Cézanne that is so admired and studied and one could be forgiven for not identifying it as such. It gives clear evidence of the struggle that Cézanne endured in the process of developing his art.

PLATE 3
Achille Emperaire (1869–70)
Oil on canvas, 78³/₄ x 48 inches (200 x 122cm)

Emperaire was a painter friend of Cézanne's and this portrait reveals him as a small, wistful and uncertain figure seated in a pretentious chair. There is no evidence of any animosity between the two, but it hardly seems an affectionate portrayal though the two were good friends for at least ten years. The effect of the composition is curious, the reason being that Emperaire was a dwarf with a large head and a thin body and limbs. Cézanne later described him as 'a burning soul, nerves of steel, an iron pride in a misshapen body, a flame of genius in a crooked hearth'. Cézanne made preparatory drawings for the portrait which shows Emperaire much as Cézanne has described him, one drawing carrying within it almost the vitality of a Bernini sketch.

one speaker complained that it was sad that few art students could explain what the central core of Cézanne's work was, at which the chairman opined that he himself was not sure that he could, and to complete the circle the speaker himself confessed that he was not sure he could either. This may act as a salutary warning. Most students of Cézannes's work agree that it was seminally important and are able to adduce reasons, make perceptive comments, examine the effect of associations, explain his technique, quote his own observations on art and analyse his paintings; but even when aggregated, these elements do not fully explain the reverence and establish the pre-eminence in which he is held. There is a revealing 'for instance'. He is often claimed to have been the principal influence in the origins of Cubism (which he undoubtedly was), but in establishing this, a line written by Cézanne to Émile Bernard in 1904 is often quoted: ' ... treat nature by the cone, sphere and cylinder.' Not, one notes, the cube. But throughout Cézanne's work, the sense of a structural geometry is evident as well as the careful and tentative

intellectual underbuilding towards what he called his *motif* – his *petite sensation*. Nonetheless, shorn of all the academic, scholarly dissection and aesthetic hype, the fact remains that Cézanne has been accorded a place in the hierarchy of art above that of almost all his peers.

To understand why this has happened, and before we attempt to evaluate his qualities and achievements, the background to the development of the art of the 19th century may be helpful. Cézanne was born in 1839. His most significant close contemporaries were born respectively, Pissarro in 1831, Manet in 1832, Degas in 1834, Monet in 1840, Renoir in 1841, Gauguin in 1848, Van Gogh in 1853, Seurat in 1859 and, before Cézanne died in 1906, Matisse in 1869 and Picasso in 1881. When Cézanne was born, the important Neo-Classical movement established by Jacques-Louis David and reaching its apogee in the work of Jean-Auguste-Dominique Ingres, who died in 1867, still dominated the French Salon. By the time he was an adult, Romanticism and the important work of Delacroix, who died in 1863, a year highly significant in French art, had begun to inspire young painters, and independent anti-classical groups were beginning to form.

In 1863, when Cézanne was 24 and living in the south of France, the Salon des Refusés – in which Manet exhibited what was thought to be a scandalous and obscene painting, *Le déjeuner sur l'herbe* – signalled the beginning of

PLATE 4
Head of an Old Man (1865–68)
Oil on canvas, 20 x 18⁷/₈ inches (51 x 48cm)

The characteristics mentioned in the note to plate 2 apply again here, although there are some discernible qualities which will lead to Cézanne's later work; the forehead, for instance, is modelled in a way that shows an interest in expressing the strong dome-like form of the skull. The way the clothes are painted, coarsely and vigorously but incompletely, reveals that Cézanne has painted over another painting, leaving the right lower corner unpainted. (It represents a procession of some kind, as can be discerned by turning the painting on its side.) A painter who at this time sat for a portrait by him, wrote, in a letter to Émile Zola, that 'every time Cézanne paints one of his friends he seems to avenge himself for some hidden injury'.

what was to become the Impressionist Revolution in which Cézanne was marginally and temporarily to participate. It might be noted here that much difficulty and confusion has been caused in trying to include Cézanne as an Impressionist – both to an understanding of Impressionism and to Cézanne himself. It is perhaps wiser to assess Cézanne's real achievement in the period after Impressionism.

In 1870, the Franco-Prussian War between France and Germany began, resulting in the Siege of Paris, changes in the nature of French government, the redesign of the centre of Paris by Baron Haussmann and the dispersion of the art community from the capital – all with considerable cultural damage and disruption. After the war, the Salon reopened and artistic life revived in Paris so that in 1874 the first Impressionist exhibition was held. Reluctantly, and championed only by Pissarro, his friend, Cézanne was admitted but showed only three works. Nevertheless, he was a focus of the most vitriolic criticism for an exhibition which was generally unsuccessful and a critical disaster. Manet, then the leader of those young independents who organized the show, refused to exhibit because Cézanne had been admitted (at that time he had no regard either for Cézanne or his work) and never thereafter showed in the succeeding seven Impressionist exhibitions. Of the three works Cézanne exhibited, *The House of the Hanged Man* (plate 7) is the most significant.

Despite the ridicule, this was the beginning of a series of eight exhibitions (the last in 1886), by which time the Impressionists were recognized and successful; behind their success was the beginning of a development which has become known accurately though not descriptively as Post-Impressionism. This name was surprisingly coined in 1911 by the English painter, critic and writer, and a member of the Bloomsbury group, Roger Fry. Fry himself described it as a 'somewhat negative label' for the exhibition he staged of modern French art at the Grafton Galleries to fill a blank in its programme. It was very successful despite the expectations of its organizers and the fact that Fry was not very familiar with the work he was proposing to exhibit. He visited a number of Paris galleries and dealers, including Ambroise Vollard, Cézanne's dealer, whom he already knew. When it came to naming the exhibition and after discarding a number of suggestions, Fry described it precisely in the phrase: 'Oh let's call them Post-Impressionists; at any event they came after the Impressionists.' The name has stuck and has usually been applied to the generation of younger painters as well as to the later work of some Impressionists. The exhibition, named 'Manet and the Post-Impressionists', opened on 8 November 1910. Manet was Fry's starting-point, although perhaps more appropriately to be described as a Pre- rather than Post-Impressionist, and nine of his works were included. But it was Gauguin (49 works), Van Gogh (25)

PLATE 5
A Modern Olympia (1872–73) below
Oil on canvas, 18 x 21²/₃ inches (46 x 55cm)

A Modern Olympia *represents the exotic element in Cézanne's
character which led him into curious historicist exercises. This
painting parodies Manet's* Olympia, *the scandalous work
exhibited in the 1865 Salon, and it achieved an almost equal
succès de scandale at the first Impressionist exhibition in 1874.
It was one of the three works included and it was because of
Cézanne's inclusion that Manet did not exhibit himself. One
comment was: 'Cézanne merely gives the impression of being a
sort of madman who paints in "delirium tremens".' It was the
last outburst of baroque excess as far as the youthful Cézanne
was concerned.*

PLATE 6
Still-Life with Green Pot and Pewter Jug
(1869–70) opposite
Oil on canvas, 25¹/₃ x 31⁷/₈ inches (64.5 x 81cm)

This painting, together with another from the same time, The
Black Clock, *has usually been identified with the change in
Cézanne's technique that was leading to the development of his
own style and direction. Although during the 1870s he was
associated with the Impressionists under Pissarro's influence,
unlike them he retained a dominant interest in the still-life as a
subject, while they were more interested in landscape or genre
subjects. For him, the 'grappling directly with objects',
undemanding and unchanging, with only the form and
relationship to be considered, was a sufficiently inspiring task.
While these early works do not perhaps have the grandeur and
deeply signifying unity of his mature still-life paintings, they do
unmistakably indicate the way his art was moving – away from
baroque romanticism to a classical silence.*

and Cézanne (21) who made up the bulk of the large exhibition. The 20th century was also represented in the works of Fauvists Marquet, Manguin, Vlaminck, Derain and Matisse and Picasso were also included. It is significant that this was the first conjunction of the 19th- and 20th-century forward-looking movements and Cézanne was an important, if posthumous, participant.

There is one perhaps appropriate justification for the title Post-Impressionist as applied to the reaction to Impressionism occurring in the 1880s in that the character of the work of even the acknowledged Impressionists was from that time beginning to change – or already had done so. There were two particular ways in which this might be described: one 'scientifically analytical', the other 'emotionally significant'. Of the four most important (the other three being Seurat, Van Gogh and Gauguin), it is Cézanne who most clearly establishes the potential future programme for the remainder of the 19th and into the 20th century and that gives him his acknowledged pre-eminence. As we have noted earlier, his background and character seemed an unlikely presage of things to come.

Paul Cézanne was born on 19 January 1839 in Aix-en-Provence. His father, Louis-Auguste, was a local hatter who with some enterprise, acumen and good luck had established a successful business in the felt-manufacturing town of Aix-en-Provence just before the boom in felt hats for men and women occurred. He was shrewd and business-like and with two partners had a shop in the main street of Aix. He made a considerable fortune, eventually becoming one of the richest men in town. With this, his ambition increased and, realizing that he could profit more from lending money than selling hats, took the opportunity of buying the local bank when it failed and, under his control, this in turn flourished. Despite his success he was not socially accepted in the town because he had committed the cardinal sin of taking a mistress in the 1830s. Anne-Élisabeth-Honorine Aubert, 16 years Louis-Auguste's junior, became Paul's mother and two years later another child, Marie, was born. A further two years elapsed before Louis-Auguste married Anne and ten years later they had their third and last child, Rose. The Cézannes, even after they had established a regular

PLATE 7
The House of the Hanged Man, Auvers
(1873)
Oil on canvas, 21⅞ x 26¼ inches (55.5 x 66.5cm)

This painting was also exhibited in the first Impressionist exhibition and a comparison with A Modern Olympia (plate 5) shows how far Cézanne had come under the influence of Pissarro with whom he had worked in Pontoise in the previous year. This is a considered and objective study, so remarkably different as to seem out of character in such a stubborn person as Cézanne – in fact, Zola once claimed that, 'to convince Cézanne of anything is like teaching the towers of Nôtre-Dame to dance'. The picture, which depicts an attractive house, is of more solid construction than a characteristic 'Impressionist' work might be and, included with them, is already an indication of Cézanne's more pictorially structured work. Although called the house of the hanged man, there is no record of any association with such a person. At that time, Cézanne spent most of the year in Auvers and made daily visits to Pissarro in Pontoise.

conjugal relationship, remained social outsiders. Louis-Auguste became a recluse though he was loved and admired by his children despite being rejected by the town. Unable and unwilling to reveal or express his emotions, he passed his own lack of self-confidence on to his children, a characteristic which Paul retained throughout his life and which led to many of his actions being misinterpreted.

After a primary education in Aix, Paul became a boarder at the Collège Bourbon where he at first suffered greatly from bullying which, since he was large and strong he overcame, though not without further damage to his self-esteem. At college he made a friend who had a considerable affect upon his life both then and later. Émile Zola, whose father had been an engineer in Aix and had died when Émile was seven, was left almost destitute when his mother failed to recover the substantial monies owed to her husband for engineering work already completed. Émile was sent as a part boarder to the college and, unlike Paul, was small, sharp and outspoken and had not been born in Aix – all crimes according to the young school bullies. Cézanne championed him and the tormenters eventually left Zola alone, so beginning a lifetime relationship which was subject to many vicissitudes and, eventually, a break-up. In 1858, Zola left for Paris and Paul entered the drawing academy in Aix. In the following year, Louis-Auguste bought the country house near Aix

PLATE 8
Dr. Gachet's House in Auvers (c. 1873)
Oil on canvas, 18 x 14³/₄ inches (46 x 37.5cm)

In April 1872, Dr. Gachet bought a property in the rue Rémy in Auvers and Cézanne spent the whole of 1873 in the town with Hortense and their son Jean, making daily trips on foot to Pontoise where he worked with Pissarro who, it will be recalled, Cézanne regarded as his teacher. It was during this period that Cézanne, under Pissarro's influence, came closest to being an Impressionist but (as can be seen here) the structure and geometry of the picture is already significant to him.

PLATE 9
Flowers in a Delft Vase (c. 1873–75)
Oil on canvas, 16 x 10²/₃ inches (41 x 27cm)

PLATE 10
Dahlias (c.1873–75)
Oil on canvas, 28³/₄ x 21¹/₄ inches (73 x 54cm)

Painted in Auvers at Dr. Gachet's house, this was retained by the Gachet family until it was donated by them, together with Flowers in a Delft Vase (below left), and entered the Louvre collection of Impressionism in 1951. Dr. Gachet was an amateur painter himself, exhibiting under the pseudonym of Van Ryssel, and was a friend of Cézanne and other painters, including Van Gogh, who committed suicide while in his care. The dense impasto of this painting, different from the earlier palette-knife applications, is the result of the influence of the remarkable painter Monticelli who became Cézanne's friend, introduced to him by Pissarro. There is a richly manipulated colour quality, given its key by the vibrant white flowers.

PLATE 11
Self-Portrait (c. 1875)
Oil on canvas, 25¼ x 20½ inches (64 x 52cm)

It was only during the 1870s that Cézanne made a number of self-portraits, although there are some drawings and one painting from 1861–62. This one is probably the first of these, although it

is difficult to establish a precise chronology. It is an interesting mixture of Cézanne's early and developing approach to paint application. A number of the brushstrokes are forceful and strongly, if vaguely, a directional harking back, while the structure of the dome of the head is painted with searching care; it was a constant preoccupation in his portraits. The painting behind the head is part of an urban scene by Guillaumin, another close friend.

known as Jas de Bouffan around which Cézanne centred much of his early work. Also in 1859, on the instructions of his father, he unhappily and unwillingly began to study law at the University of Aix. But he was now already determined to become a painter and in 1861 he abandoned his law studies and made his first visit to Paris where he met Pissarro, already a professional painter and part of the independent group, at the Atelier Suisse, one of the well known Parisian studios in which professional painters taught the process of painting in the academic tradition. After the first meeting, Pissarro described Cézanne as a 'curious Provençal' – an early example of the effect Cézanne had on anyone meeting him for the first time. Despite first impressions, Pissarro remained a friend and early mentor to Cézanne.

After this visit, Cézanne, under parental pressure, returned to work in his father's bank; but his ambition to become a painter dominated his thoughts and feelings. He took up painting and returned to Paris where he failed entrance to the École des Beaux Arts, was rejected for the Salon every year from 1864 to 1869, and worked in the Atelier Suisse. This unpropitious beginning in a city which was the centre of European artistic life was discouraging, and his relative naïvety and retiring manner did little to further his progress. Nevertheless he persisted, and remained based in Paris until the outbreak of the Franco-Prussian War in 1870, making occasional visits to Aix. As

has been noted, he exhibited in the Salon des Refusés in 1863 and was a peripheral figure in the group that met at the Café Guerbois and of which Manet was the leader. He had been introduced by Pissarro who was at that time almost his only strong supporter.

At the outbreak of the war, and to escape from army service, Cézanne went to L'Estaque in 1870, living there with a model, Hortense Fiquet, where their son Paul was born in January 1872. In this year Cézanne went to work with Pissarro in Pontoise, coming under his influence and changing his early heavy pigmental style to a near Impressionist technique. Although this influence was short-lived, it gave Cézanne contact with the Impressionists although only Pissarro regarded him highly. He was beginning to achieve some small reputation as a serious painter, though thought by his peers to be technically unaccomplished, but failed to sell his work and lived off a small allowance from his unconvinced father.

The first Impressionist exhibition opened in the former studio of the famous photographer Nadar on 15 April 1874. Organized by Degas and Monet, it included three paintings by Cézanne of which one, *The House of the Hanged Man* (plate 7), was bought by Comte Doria. After the close of the exhibition a month later, Cézanne spent short periods in Aix and Paris, returning to Aix and thence to L'Estaque. He declined to exhibit in the second Impressionist show (1876) but in the third held

PLATE 12
Three Bathers (1879–82)
Oil on canvas, 20$^1/_2$ x 21$^2/_3$ inches (52 x 55cm)

Matisse bought this painting from Vollard in 1899 and it was donated by him to the Petit Palais in 1936. It has acquired a critical importance in the study of the influence of Cézanne on 20th-century painting. As already noted in the introduction,

Matisse was a great admirer and at the time of donating the work wrote to the curator: 'Permit me [to say] that this picture is of the first importance in Cézanne's oeuvre, for it is the very dense and very complete realization much studied by him in several canvases which, although in important collections, are only the studies that led up to this work.' These series paintings which continued to the end of his life are a significant aspect of Cézanne's method. (See also plates 45 and 46.)

PLATE 13
Self-Portrait (c. 1880)
Oil on canvas, 17³/₄ x 14¹/₂ inches (45 x 37cm)

As already noted, Cézanne painted a number of self-portraits and
this example from his maturity reveals how he had developed his
structural control and unity to the extent that this is one of his
finest portraits. The pictorial relationship between the smooth dome
of the solid skull and its opposite in the solid rough beard, and
the hinge of the ear that links them indissolubly, creates an image
of absolute immutability which makes the painting a separate
identity from its inspiration. It is a wonderful extension of the
nature of representation which Cézanne took forward from
Impressionism and, in turn, from the influence of the
Renaissance.

in the following year showed 16 paintings.

Although Cézanne's private life was undramatic and
he was not in great financial need, his father had
discovered his liaison with Hortense and unsuccessfully
tried to break it up. Cézanne's father, despite his financial
acumen, retained an essentially peasant attitude towards the
arts, could not comprehend his son's intellectual needs, and
was disgusted that a man of 40 was not able to support
himself. On learning of his son's unconventional domestic
situation and despite the fact that he had himself behaved
in an exactly similar manner, his father cut his allowance
from the modest 200 francs a month to 100, leaving
Cézanne impossibly little on which to support his family.
He appealed to his friend Zola to find him a job who
helped him out financially instead; Zola offered, as he said,
to help 'as long as is necessary'. Cézanne asked that the
money be sent directly to Hortense who was living in
Marseille with their son Paul who was ill.

Through Renoir, in 1875, Cézanne met Victor
Chocquet, a customs official, an amateur painter and a
collector of Impressionist paintings despite having little
money – evidence that these paintings could be bought for
no great sum of money. Cézanne painted both Chocquet's
portrait and that of his wife. Although still ridiculed by the
critics, his painter friends – encouraged by Pissarro – were
beginning to realize that this strange and diffident character
was not following the same Impressionist course as

expressed by Monet, Renoir and Pissarro, but was moving
in a personal direction of his own. By the end of the
1870s, Cézanne was spending more time in Aix and less in
Paris. He was also working with Pissarro in Pontoise,
where he met Gauguin, and in L'Estaque with Renoir. In
1883 he worked for most of the year around Aix and later
the same year, in December, was joined in the south by
Monet and Renoir. By 1885, he was in Aix or L'Estaque
for most of the year to begin a more settled and
undramatic period of painting.

The year 1886 was an important one for Cézanne.
The last Impressionist exhibition took place in which
Cézanne exhibited paintings. For Cézanne, it was the end
of an annual event which had become too closely
identified with what by then was a popular movement and
with which many lesser artists had become associated; it no
longer had any relevance to Cézanne or his work which,
even from the first, had not truly represented his views.
From this time, Cézanne came to be recognized for what
he had always been – an individualist in search of his own
language.

Three developments in Cézanne's personal life were
also of great significance in the same year. Firstly, Zola
published his novel *L'Oeuvre*, which caused a rift in his
relationship with Cézanne who was deeply hurt by
obvious, if not explicit, uncomplimentary references to
himself in the central character, Claude Lantier, a painter.

PLATE 14
Female Nude on Sofa (c.1880–82)
Oil on canvas, 16$^1/_2$ x 24 inches (42 x 61cm)

This curious work is part of a study for Cézanne's painting of
Leda and the Swan *and includes at a different scale two pears*
in the top left-hand corner. In the eventual painting, Leda is in
the same pose and the Swan replaces the pears. This is
Cézanne's version of a voluptuous nude, structured as a
landscape or still-life might have been. The result is a somewhat
incongruous figure, the doubtless sagging flesh bound into a strict
architecture. In the final work, the swan is biting Leda's raised
hand. Cézanne was making other nudes studies at this time –
usually of male bathers.

PLATE 15
The Château at Médan (c. 1880) detail
Oil on canvas, 23¼ x 28⅓ inches (59 x 72cm)

Émile Zola, as the result of the success of his novel,
L'Assommoir, *was able to buy a house at Médan, near Paris.
Naturally Cézanne, his friend, was invited to visit on frequent
occasions and during one visit he painted a château from a small
island in the Seine that Zola owned. (Zola's house is to the right
of the château and not visible in the painting.) As in the two
still-life paintings illustrated in plates 16 and 17, this work is in
three tonal bands, ranging from the deepest upwards to the
lightest. Within the central band there is another which contains
the outbuildings of the château with the main building on the
right and the vertical trees interrupting the flow of the straggling
buildings and providing a tight, interlocked composition. The trees
piercing the sky enliven the control and is a frequent solution for
Cézanne.*

Secondly, he married Hortense in the presence of both his
parents which restored their damaged relationship. Thirdly,
and later in the same year, his father died, leaving Cézanne
an appreciable fortune.

Cézanne's reputation was beginning to grow despite
his reclusive life in the south of France and in 1889
Chocquet arranged to have the painting, *La Maison du
Pendu* (*The House of the Hanged Man*) shown at the Paris
World Fair. In the same year he exhibited in Belgium. His
new financial independence enabled him to settle Hortense
and their son in Aix, leaving him to pursue his painting
wherever he wished. Although well known, his isolation
from the centre of artistic life (which was of his own
choosing) was turning him into something of a remote and
legendary figure. In 1894 he spent the summer at Giverny
on the Seine near Paris, the famous home of Monet and
the haunt of artists and notable figures in French arts,
culture and society. There he met Clemenceau, the great
political figure known as the 'Tiger of France', Auguste
Rodin, Mary Cassatt (the American Impressionist friend of
Degas) and Gustave Geffroy, the critic and writer.

A young American painter, Matilda Lewis, who was
staying at the same hotel as Cassatt and Cézanne in
Giverny, provides us with a graphic description and
character analysis of Cézanne at that time. Quoting
Daudet's description of the man from the Midi as 'a man

Continued on page 180

PLATE 16
Still-Life with Apples and Biscuits
(c.1877–80)
Oil on canvas, 15 x 21²/₃ inches (38 x 55cm)

This careful composition, divided horizontally into three near equal bands of different tonal values (the lowest in the centre) is contrived to establish a calm balance of simple elements within the central band, only enlivened by the harsh darks in the lower and the delicate shapes in the upper. It is a subject that Cézanne repeats a number of times around the end of the 1870s. One critic wrote: ' ...this still-life is among the purest of Cézanne's maturity, one of those that best sums up the essential characteristics of his art in his most serene period.' The calm presentation of these unimportant objects gives them a quality of inevitability, the sense of complete harmony for which Cézanne was always searching.

PLATE 17
Still-Life with Apples and Biscuits (c.1880)
overleaf
Oil on canvas, 18 x 21²/₃ inches (46 x 55cm)

A comparison with the previous illustration will indicate where Cézanne's interest lies. It is not in the objects depicted, nor their disposition on the surface, but lies in a determination to discover an immanent relationship in the area of the canvas and his vision of it as a captured harmony. He has three bands again, but of different proportions, which lay emphasis on the central white cloth which supports the apples. He has introduced a dynamic relationship in the opposition of the circular apples and the star decorations of the wallpaper, while a solid band of deep-red apples balances the dancing lighter ones.

Continued from page 174

with large red eyeballs standing out from his head in a most ferocious manner' as her first impression, she goes on to admit that she had misjudged him by his appearance since he had, in fact, 'the gentlest manner possible, *comme un enfant*'. She was startled by his table manners: he scraped his soup plate and poured the dregs into his spoon and tore the meat from his chop with his fingers. Cézanne was also sensitive to what he regarded as a slight or ridicule and his visit to Giverny ended abruptly in the middle of a meal when he suspected his friends, who had actually been making complimentary remarks about his work, were laughing at him. He returned immediately to Aix without even informing Monet, who nevertheless returned several canvases that Cézanne had left at the hotel in his haste. They never met again. A further indication of Cézanne's provincial small-town attitude is revealed in his first meeting with Rodin when he knelt to kiss Rodin's hand, not because he was a great sculptor but because he had been awarded the Légion d'Honneur.

In the following year, Ambroise Vollard, the dealer

PLATE 18
Poplars (1879–82)
Oil on canvas, 25½ x 31⅞ inches (65 x 81cm)

The sensation of poplars is, as Monet too has demonstrated, their verticality and in the mass they produce a green density, punctuated by thin lines which are vertical, or nearly so. Cézanne's development, by about 1880, had introduced what became a characteristic and identifying means of applying paint in parallel brushstrokes. He has used the verticals, as he usually does, as stabilizing elements in a combination with parallel brushstrokes in opposing directional blocks. The two slim trees on the left edge are the spatially defining elements against the curving path, giving an overall effect of a rich and verdant landscape. The location has been identified as just north of Pontoise where Cézanne had been living at the time.

PLATE 19
The Aqueduct (1885–87) detail
Oil on canvas, 35³/₄ x 28¹/₃ inches (91 x 72cm)

The aqueduct in the Arc valley below Mont Sainte-Victoire appears in many of Cézanne's paintings, executed when he was in Aix. One of his vantage points was the farm owned by his

sister, Rose, and it is from here that most of the famous paintings of Mont Sainte-Victoire, now one of the most familiar views in Western painting, were produced. In this painting, the so-called aqueduct provides the stabilizing horizontal in the painting of trees near Bellevue. The extraordinary vitality of the tree-trunks invests the whole painting with a life that is essentially pictorial, that is to say internal.

PLATE 20
Still-Life with Fruits, Napkin and Milk Jug
(c. 1879–82)
Oil on canvas, 23²/₃ x 28¹/₃ inches (60 x 72cm)

Painted in the location of the still-life in plate 17, this composition is almost equally and horizontally divided, but it will be noticed that a curious 'inaccuracy' has been introduced. The far edge to the left of the napkin does not follow the line of the rear edge on the right. Some explanation of this seems necessary: the suggestion of incompetence that may immediately come to mind cannot be sustained when Cézanne's concern with the total picture area is recalled. Why then? – if one also recalls that Cézanne is searching always for a unity and harmony, not the simple reproduction of the scene. If one considers moving the rear-edge line either up or down, one realizes that the delicate balance of the structure of relationships would fall apart; the milk jug would lose its identity, for instance. It is a major part of Cézanne's significance for later painters that he is creating a non-adjustable pictorial object.

that supported him, organized his first exhibition of Cézanne's work, having been encouraged to do so by Pissarro; Cézanne showed 150 paintings – a fair indication of his dedication to his art since he was a slow worker. An example of this is revealed in a reported conversation between them while Vollard was being painted by Cézanne. After 115 sittings, Vollard, not unnaturally perhaps, enquired how the painting was progressing and Cézanne replied, 'I am not displeased with the shirt front.' (See plate 41.) This remains not only an indication of Cézanne's way of working but the seriousness of the reply is a clue to his character.

Gustave Caillebotte, a painter and collector who had died two years earlier, had made a great collection of paintings including Impressionist works, and had left it to the State. Renoir was his executor and had some trouble persuading the authorities to accept the legacy. Ultimately, in 1895, 65 of the works came to the national collection. Of the five by Cézanne, only two were accepted by the directors and entered the Luxembourg Museum collection. Later, Vollard bought the entire collection of work in one of Cézanne's studios. It had been a slow progress and Cézanne was by no means universally admired or widely understood but by the end of the century he was recognized by many as a master, a fact evidenced by the painting *Hommage à Cézanne* which Maurice Denis, a

PLATE 21.

Mont Sainte-Victoire with Large Pine
(1886–87)

Oil on canvas, 23½ x 28½ inches (59.7 x 72.5cm)

From this same location near the farm Bellevue, Cézanne painted most of his grand views of the mountain that dominated the scene and occupied his mind through the 1880s. What may be declared, however, is that the paintings of this subject produced during the 1880s are part of the most mature and inspiring of what is called his 'classical' period and carry the same authority as great masterpieces from such painters as Poussin. The scene itself is interesting. Cézanne's raised view from Bellevue is across the valley of the river Arc (on the banks of which Cézanne and Zola played as children) to the dominating Mont Sainte-Victoire, named, it is said, in honour of a victory by the Romans over the barbarians in the first century A.D. From his vantage point, the plain stretches uninterrupted to the mountain providing Cézanne with the sort of pictorial problem which would have engaged and delighted him. He was concerned with two things which he described as his motif *and his* petite sensation. *The* motif *was the identity of the subject; the* petite sensation *was its individual special quality. While admitting that this is a simplification of what Cézanne would also call a process of 'logic', it does perhaps indicate that the result would, if successful, be a simple pictorial statement in only its own terms. It is, incidentally, another example of a landscape bisected by a rail line of which the viaduct is the evident reminder. For the Impressionist painters, the train and its implications was a symbol of the impact of modern life upon the historic landscape, evidence of which is seen in the work of Monet, Renoir, Pissarro, Degas, as well as Cézanne.*
(See also plates 42, 43 and 44.)

PLATE 22
The Bay of Marseille seen from L'Estaque
(1882–85)

Oil on canvas, 22³/₄ x 28¹/₃ inches (58 x 72cm)

Cézanne painted this subject a number of times from different viewpoints, some more distant, giving emphasis to the vertical smoke tower seen here in the foreground. He was particularly attracted by the strength in the middle-distance of the bay itself, a flat area of colour in the middle of the picture area with strong forms in the far distance and foreground. Although at first examination this painting may suggest that it is Impressionist in character, it is actually more in keeping with the investigations that Cézanne was making into pictorial identity and the sea area enables him to construct his 'flat' space above and below to connect the picture plane. It shows an assurance in structured composition of his later work. The painting of the hills and shore in the background is particularly effective when one recalls how a photograph of a distant range of hills appears as a very small area while making a powerful visual impact.

PLATE 23
Pierrot and Harlequin (1888)
Oil on canvas, 40¼ x 31⅞ inches (102 x 81cm)

Also called 'Mardi Gras', this is an unusual painting in the Cézanne oeuvre. Cézanne made a number of studies for it and a painting of the Harlequin figure alone, but it did not presage a series. According to Paul, Cézanne's son, he posed for the Harlequin figure and his great friend Louis Guillaume, son of a cobbler, for Pierrot. At the time, Paul was 16 and if the story is true he seems to have been a singularly self-assured youth. They are in commedia dell'arte *costume and it is interesting to note that other painters subsequently chose similar subjects, including Picasso. Cézanne was in Paris when the work was painted and had inherited from his father's estate, giving him a financial freedom which opened up new possibilities, including the ability to pay for professional models. It is also apparent that he had acquired a new interest in the figure and portraiture after many years of concentrating on landscapes and still-lifes.*

member of the Nabis group, exhibited at the Salon of 1901. In 1899 Jas de Bouffan was sold to settle the family estate on the death of Cézanne's mother, and although he had attempted to buy the Château Noir where he had been painting, he failed and worked in various rented premises until 1902 when he moved to the new studio he had built on the Chemin des Lauves at Aix.

In 1902 Émile Bernard published a pamphlet on Cézanne. Zola died in September of the same year, unreconciled with Cézanne who was nevertheless deeply upset and Vollard reports Cézanne weeping at the mention of Zola's name. Pissarro followed in 1903, a close friend to the last. (Cézanne later described himself, in the catalogue of an exhibition in 1906, as a 'pupil of Pissarro'.) In October 1904 at the Second Salon d'Automne in Paris, an entire room containing 31 paintings and two drawings was devoted to Cézanne's work and he is listed as one of the Salon's founding members. Moreover, in October 1906, another ten Cézannes were included in the famous Salon d'Automne which included the work of the Fauve painters, Matisse, Derain and Vlaminck, members of the first of the 20th-century art movements and which reflected the influence of Cézanne. He himself was by that time seriously ill.

The summer had been very hot and Cézanne had been working in the open-air from dawn while ill with diabetes and undergoing what he describes as an 'atrocious'

course of treatment, including massage from his gardener Vallier. By August he was suffering from an attack of bronchitis but continued working through August and September and into the next month until, on 15 October he collapsed, remaining in the rain for several hours before being brought back on a laundry cart. Despite his, by then, evidently critical condition, he worked the next day in his studio on a portrait of Vallier. His condition deteriorated and five days later on the 22 October 1906 he died. In the exhibition in Aix-en-Provence when he describes himself as a pupil of Pissarro, he was showing the first and last of his works in his birthplace. The painting of the gardener Vallier, unfinished, was his last work.

THE PAINTINGS
Before considering Cézanne's work, there are some general observations that should be made which are specially, although not uniquely, applicable to him and his work.

It is evident in the work of the Impressionists, and indeed most painters after them in this century, that they were not specifically concerned with representing their subjects to a 'photographic' degree. They assumed an independence which allowed them a selective freedom, a choice of emphasis, a use of colour and way of applying paint which neither finitely identifies the forms of objects nor their local surface colour.

PLATE 24
The Card Players (c. 1893)
Oil on canvas, 17³/₄ x 22¹/₂ inches (45 x 57cm)

Cézanne painted a short series of five paintings of this subject, in two of which he included other figures. The main element in these paintings is the relaxed concentration and direct opposition of the two protagonists. Cézanne is not interested in presenting an emotional scene but is attempting to achieve with the balanced interaction of the two central figures a pictorial, tensioned structure. The off-verticals of the table-legs, together with the off-horizontals of the table-top, introduce a tension that also adds to the pictorial structure.

The Impressionists had, to this extent at least, initiated a revolution which in its outcome had a profound effect on attitudes to painting, firstly in France and eventually throughout the world. It was no mean achievement for young painters who were, in the main, still students when the need for urgent changes in painting attitudes and methods began to dominate their thinking. They were not a unified group with set aims and clear direction. They did not think of themselves as Impressionists – some in fact never did – but they did wish to be independent enough to paint as they felt. This was not what they were being taught, nor what they saw in exhibitions or at the Salon to which all professional painters wished to submit their work and have it shown. Salon works were linked indissolubly to the historical tradition of both technique and subject. The technique was tied to the Renaissance-defined, if also refined and subtle, representation of form through line or edge. The areas within were identified with a local colour, the colour of the subject (whether a body or some object) being modified by the addition of lighter or darker tone to identify volume. This admittedly simplistic description of what became, in the hands of the great painters and even able practitioners, a technique of almost unlimited flexibility and variety during the later 17th and 18th centuries (in the later years of the 18th century and early 19th it became the style known as Neo-Classicism), turned again to defined form and local colour which became the

PLATE 25
Man Smoking a Pipe (c. 1892)
Oil on canvas, 28³/₄ x 23²/₃ inches (73 x 60cm)

The subject of this work is the same person who appears as the figure on the left in The Card Players *in plate 24. He was Cézanne's gardener, Vallier, who was also the subject of the last painting Cézanne was working on when he died. This is one of the portraits that he painted in the late 1880s and early 1890s. Like many of his works, particularly of this period, the painting is unfinished in that small areas of the canvas have been left uncovered. Despite this, the work seems complete in its statement and this is a reminder that Cézanne insisted that each small stroke was significant and until he could identify what it should be he could not place it in the painting. (For an elaboration of this point, see the note to his portrait of Ambroise Vollard, his dealer and friend, in plate 41.)*

standard practice for Salon work.

The subject-matter was also clearly identified in the Salon. The 'important' works were of an intellectually 'elevated' character, dealing with significant historical or religious subjects designed for an 'educated' taste. A nude was not a nude but a Venus or Hercules. Landscapes were admitted and, although still-life paintings were accepted, they were not considered of the highest order and were required to be of a traditional character and technique.

The young independents found these limitations unacceptable and looked for alternatives. They found them in the work of Courbet, the Barbizon painters and Delacroix. An adequate consideration of their work is not possible within the limited space available here, but it is important to recognize that each was outside the academic tradition; the Barbizan painters, deeply enamoured with the local landscape around the Forest of Fontainebleau, and painting in the open-air; Courbet concerned with the dignity and poverty of the peasant life of his village, Ornans; Delacroix, the great figure of the Romantic opposition to Classicism and a painter whose attitude, painting technique and different subject-matter had the greatest impact on the young independent painters. One of his subjects *Women of Algiers* was much admired by the young painters and is a romantic parallel to Ingres' 'Turkish harem'.

By the 1860s, the conditions for an artistic revolution

PLATE 26
The Smoker (c. 1892)
Oil on canvas, 36¹/₄ x 28³/₄ inches (92 x 73cm)

The sitter appears in the Card Players series and has been identified as a labourer who worked at Jas de Bouffan called Alexandre Paullin. He is depicted in the kitchen or studio of the house with his elbow on what appears to be either the top of a ribbed chest or a patterned tablecloth. To the left, there is a grey flue pipe which holds the left side and concentrates the composition on the head, arm and strong worker's hand. The sitter seems relaxed and is quizzically regarding the artist and viewer, certainly a far cry from art critic Louis Vauxcelle's comment that Cézanne painted 'the heads of shifty obstinate peasants'. Cezanne made a preparatory drawing showing the man leaning on a table-top and it seems that Cézanne changed his intention in this area, as a line continuing the table-top can be discerned in the painting. The drawing was once in the possession of Gertrude Stein, in Paris, and it is more than probable that her artist friends, which included Matisse and Picasso, would have seen it.

PLATES 27 and 27a above
The interior and exterior of Cézanne's studio in Aix-en-Provence

PLATE 28 opposite
An elderly Cézanne in his studio while working on the *Large Bathers*

existed and were given focus by the paintings of Édouard Manet whose developing technique was of such importance that with two notorious works, *Le déjeuner sur l'herbe* (1863) and *Olympia* (1865) he became the leader, if somewhat reluctantly, of the independents who were to become the Impressionists. He did not, as has been noted, exhibit in their first exhibition in 1874, or in the subsequent seven that took place.

As we have seen in looking at his life, Cézanne was involved with the group and, under the influence of Pissarro, was for a short time associated with Impressionism. His importance is, however, not in his short-lived Impressionist period, but in the work he later produced; it would not be inappropriate to describe it as anti-Impressionist although it is more usually described as Post-Impressionist – accurately because it was later than Impressionism, but unhelpfully since it says nothing about either the quality or nature of his work.

It is perhaps of some value here to remember that life is a process of change, of advance or regression, of heightening sensitivities or stolid contentment, of descent into mediocrity or, for a few, triumphant achievement. What is certain is that humanity does not start at the highest level of accomplishment – it is attained. The artist, in almost every case, progresses from tentative beginnings towards his or her ultimate goal, passing through many stages in the process.

Cézanne's importance lies more in the work produced after the Impressionist phase rather than before or in it. And that achievement is linked more with this century than with the previous one. It is what Cézanne did after Impressionism that constitutes his major importance. It is likely that, had he not come so positively under the influence of Pissarro when he did, he would not have been an Impressionist at all. That is not to diminish Pissarro's importance to Cézanne because Pissarro had an ordered programme and clear ideas concerning the nature of painting that went beyond Impressionism and which were more in keeping with Cézanne's temperament. This is not to claim that Cézanne had a coherent programme although he was both tentative and deliberate as his work developed.

He was dedicated to his work, sensitive, easily offended, protective but unsure of his ideas, convinced of his art and with a belief that it would be eventually recognized – a belief justified in his lifetime. He was fortunate in that, from early in his career, he had supporters – even indeed, when he was an unsuccessful pupil in Aix. It is also important to remind ourselves that although for a time he was confined by a reduced allowance from his father, he was never actually forced to work for a living; painting could and did remain the entire focus of his energies and his later concentration was not distracted by financial worries.

The paintings that Cézanne's name generally recall are not his early works, which are interesting more for their potential than for what they accomplished. At the time, they occasioned pitying rather than vitriolic criticism and it is a measure of the sensitivity of some of his friends and one or two collectors who bought his work that this potential was recognized. He had begun his art studies in Aix without any marked success. He went to the Free Drawing School in 1857 and worked there until he arrived in Paris in 1861 where he met Pissarro and began his professional career. His work at the Free School was undistinguished and academic studies of the nude in pencil show him to have been capable of what most students manage to achieve but usually do not surpass. There are some drawings from the early 1860s which indicate the development of a heavy, coarse drawing style which, during the 1860s, he continued in his early oil paintings. He was probably in Paris throughout the whole of 1863 and exhibited in the Salon des Refusés with Manet's *Déjeuner*. He also studied at the Académie Suisse where, in 1861, he had met Pissarro. During the whole of this period he was working in thick impasto paint, often applied with a palette knife, on subjects ranging from nudes to still-lifes. His *Bread with Eggs* (1865), recalls both the 17th-century Spanish painters and Manet in its dark ground with highlighted objects. In the *Sugar Bowl, Pears and Blue Cup,* painted about the same time, he uses a

PLATE 29
Still-Life of Pot of Flowers and Pears
(1888–90)
Oil on canvas, 17³/₄ x 21¹/₄ inches (45 x 54cm)

In this simple still-life (as in plate 20), the far edge of the table-top is at different heights as it passes behind the objects and indeed the angle on the far right is steeper than on the left. Degas in his paintings of women bathing used the same steep perspective to draw the viewer into the painted scene. It is clear that Cézanne wanted to unify the table-top with the slanting canvas behind. It is this flattening distortion that the Cubists were later to exploit. There is a well known comment by Kandinsky in his seminal On the Spiritual in Art, *concerning Cezanne's still-life painting. 'He made a living thing out of a teacup. To be more precise, he realized the existence of a being in this cup. He raised the* nature morte *to a height where the exteriorly "dead" object becomes inwardly alive.'*

palette knife to create the forms.

Between the Salon des Refusés and the first Impressionist exhibition in 1874, Cézanne became more closely associated with the Café Guerbois group and their friends. His closest associate was Pissarro but Manet was also becoming an influence. His attachment and participation in the development of Impressionism came as late as 1872–73 while he was staying at Pontoise with Pissarro. The painting which signalled that attachment was *The House of the Hanged Man* (plate 7), mentioned earlier, where the influence of Pissarro can clearly be seen, and their discussions on the Impressionist's use of paint led to the direct change in technique in this second stage in Cézanne's development. Through the 1870s, Cézanne's Impressionism changed into an analytical examination rather than visual perception, and when he abandoned the Parisian scene in 1877 to return to Aix, his isolation and intellectual concentration, undisturbed by the artistic conversation of the café life of Paris, enabled him to pursue the *petite sensation* of his *motif*.

To understand this mature stage in his art, it is necessary to go to Cézanne's own words for clues rather than specific information since, as we have noted earlier, words will not elucidate the nature of a painter's art. Perhaps the most significant observation he made, which bears not only upon his own philosophy but has been a foundation block in much of the modern structure of taste

PLATE 30

The House of Bellevue (1890–92)

Oil on canvas, 25½ x 32 inches (64.8 x 81.2cm)

Around 1885, Maxime Conil (married to Cézanne's sister Rose) bought an estate farm called Bellevue, south-west of Aix and situated on a hill dominating the whole of the wide valley of the river Arc and looking towards Mont Sainte-Victoire. As may be imagined, it was a favourite location for Cézanne to paint and it was from here that he painted a number of his views of the great mountain and the valley. He also painted several views of the farm, the house and the pigeonnier. On the hill of Bellevue he could see a number of the motifs that engaged his interest over the years. The is one of two paintings made around the same time and reveal Cézanne's methods of construction. In the distant unfinished view, the firm lines of the picture structure are being established while the trees and shrubs surrounding the house are at an early stage of construction. The small linear strokes are suggesting further definition of the shrub forms without precluding a closer placing relating to the linear forms of the buildings. In this work, the house dominates from a close view and the relationships have been resolved in what is a complicated geometrical structure. But although the painting is well advanced there are, as usual, some small and larger areas of uncovered canvas. While Cézanne would not have considered it 'finished', in all probability he was not able to add further to the painting.

PLATE 31
The Great Pine (c.1889)
Oil on canvas, 33½ x 36¼ inches (85 x 92cm)

Joachim Gasquet was the first owner of this painting and it reminded him of walks taken with Cézanne around Aix. As will be recalled, pine trees appeared regularly in Cézanne's paintings of the area. He made a number of drawings of single pines and a few paintings of which this work is a highly impressive example. The sense of pictorial identity, the implication of this fierce life-force in pictorial form is remarkable. It has been suggested that with this single study of a pine tree, formed as much by the elements as by its life-force, Cézanne may have been thinking of the painting by Monet of a similar tree subject. (Monet was the only living painter that Cézanne actively admired.) There is information on the development of this painting. Originally the painting only contained about two-thirds of the tree, the top being cut off by the top edge; but Cézanne then felt the need to open the painting to introduce more sky and successively added two bands of canvas, which may be discerned in the reproduction.

and art criticism was: 'Art is a harmony, parallel with the harmony of nature.' This suggests that he saw art, not as a casual observation of natural form – which would not place art in parallel to the harmony of nature – but to the superficial identification of varying surface experiences which of themselves were only the accident of locality. For Cézanne, the essential structure of the picture was to be drawn from the unity (harmony) of the whole of the experience of nature as drawn out of the selected *motif*. Such a search was pictorially unrelated directly to the creation of illusionist space, accidental effects of light, temporary colour and painting technique or pigment application. The painting for him became the object carrying the message, not the landscape that sponsored it. Far from light and atmosphere fracturing form, as had been the aim of the Impressionists, for Cézanne the elemental basic volumes were his own basis for the pictorial construction of his *motif*. It is not to be supposed that he looked for underlying geometric forms on which to construct his image, as has been construed from his letter to Bernard to 'treat nature by the cylinder, the sphere, the cone', but that these should be in mind as a guide to rendering his immediate perception, which is implied when he says 'sensations form the foundation of my work'. It is important to note that the forms he suggested should be used – the cylinder, sphere and cone – are curved in movement in space, not in conjoined or

PLATE 32
The Lac d'Annecy (1896)
Oil on canvas, 25¼ x 31⅛ inches (64.2 x 79.1cm)

Cézanne sold this painting to Ambroise Vollard soon after he had completed it. It shows the Château de Duingt on the side of the lake with the hills rearing behind it. It creates a feeling of claustrophobia without the release of any sky and the strong directional strokes make the circularity of the composition around the château hub evident, emphasized by the curved implication of the tree-trunk. The verticals in this painting descend from the horizontal (rather than rise from it as is more usual) and this is another indication of the psychological effect that linear direction and relationship held for Cézanne and made explicit in Seurat's theory that 'lines descending from the horizontal give sadness'. There is certainly an air of quiet nostalgia and remoteness in this exquisite work. Cézanne stayed at the small town of Talloires, in the Savoie, near the lake, and wrote to his friend Gasquet from there, noting the height of the mountains and the lake narrowed by two gorges. Others have remarked on the daunting mountains and the deep menace of the lake. This was the only painting Cézanne completed in Talloires.

PLATE 33

Still-Life with Fruit Basket (The Kitchen Table) (c.1888–89)

Oil on canvas, 25½ x 32 inches (64.7 x 81.2cm)

*This is an unusually complex, and in some ways unresolved work
with a more than usual number of objects contained within it.
Neither the perspective nor the physical positioning are consistent.
As we have noted in other still-life paintings, the front table
corners do not conjoin and there are other curiosities; the ellipses of
the jars are at different eye-levels and the basket would not sit as
placed on the table. The chair-leg on the right and the chair in the
background do not sit in the created space. It is so different from
other still-life works in its deep spatial exploration, rather than the
usual flat wall which Cézanne places close behind his objects, that
it seems to have been inspired by a different exploratory spirit.
One could cite other instances of inconsistency or inaccuracy but
nevertheless there remains an extraordinary authority and delight
which convinces us of the pictorial rightness of the whole – what
Cézanne called 'plastic equivalents' of reality.*

integrated flat planes. His injunction to 'treat' nature is
thus one of sequential change – movement in space flatly
identified for the purposes of art. 'Painting is not only to
copy the object, it is to seize a harmony between
numerous relations.' This was for him an objective with
profound difficulties. So profound, that a single spot of
colour could unbalance the carefully constructed harmony
of the whole. As he confessed, 'I cannot attain the
intensity that is unfolded before my eyes.' This explains
why, when Vollard questioned him about two small spots
of white canvas on his hands in the portrait, Cézanne
explained that he could decide what they should be
without further reference – and they still remain
unpainted. (*See plate 41.*)

    Cézanne said, 'I advance all my canvas at one time
together.' This is so that at every stage it is as complete at
that stage as it can be – one false building block and the
edifice disintegrates or, as Cézanne puts it, 'There must
not be a single link too loose, not a crevice through which
may escape the emotion, the light, the truth.' From this
emerges the essential element in Cézanne's painting. There
is a truth which is the painting, not the subject, not the
object but the single identity of the painting which is
complete as itself – or as complete as it exists undefiled at
any stage in its growth.

    It should be said that it is this 'flat space' – the

Continued on page 213

PLATE 34
Peasant in a Blue Smock (c. 1895–1900)
Oil on canvas, 31⁷/₈ x 25¹/₂ inches (81 x 65cm)

During the later 1880s and 1890s Cézanne often used local people as models as his interest in portraiture and his devotion to his local landscape continued to engross him. Peasant in a Blue Smock is part of the Mont Sainte-Victoire landscape. This individual appears in two of the Card Players paintings and was evidently someone who in his passive stolidity interested Cézanne. He is seated here in front of what seems to be an unexpectedly elegant female carrying a parasol. In fact, it is a detail of a screen that Cézanne had painted for Jas de Bouffan many years earlier when his father first purchased the house. Some of the portraits were painted in Jas de Bouffan and it seems that Cézanne was intrigued by the relationship of the phlegmatic sitter to the unfamiliar sophistication that surrounded him. Cézanne's practice of not continuing horizontal edges, as can be noted in plate 20, is present in this painting in a different form. The left-hand edge of the smock below the arm, and its width inside the arm, do not coincide with the physical structure of the sitter; but the whole corresponds to the pictorial unity of the peasant's image. An indication that Cézanne's work was appreciated by his friends is apparent in an observation that Gasquet made when he saw the painting in Cézanne's studio: 'One especially, in a blue smock, decked out in a red foulard, his arms dangling, is admirable in his ruggedness, like the materialized thought of a bit of earth that's suddenly been incarnated in this crude and magnificent flesh, cooked by the sun and whipped by the wind.'

PLATE 35
Portrait of Madame Cézanne
(c.1885–90) detail
Oil on canvas, 31⁷/₈ x 25¹/₂ inches (81 x 65cm)

Cézanne painted his wife a number of times during their long relationship, both before and after their marriage in 1886. In these rather simple, thinly painted works, the character of a study is more evident than of a fully resolved work. This was executed when Hortense was in her late 30s and they reveal a mature woman with a peaceful nature.

It was in 1886 that Zola published his novel in which his central figure is the artist Claude Lantier, based on Cézanne. In the book, the model and wife of Lantier is Christine Hallegrin and it seems that Zola had Hortense in mind when he created the character. He describes her thus: '...a tall supple and slim girl, still a little thin in body... A brunette with black hair and black eyes. The upper part of the face very gentle, with great tenderness. Long eye-lids, pure and tender forehead, small and delicate nose... But the lower part of her face is passionate, the jaw a little prominent, too strong ...'

PLATE 36
Woman in Blue (before 1899, or 1900–04)
Oil on canvas, 34⁵/₈ x 28¹/₃ inches (88.5 x 72cm)

There is considerable uncertainty surrounding this painting. It was dated around 1895 but recently has been redated to soon after 1900 and was painted either in Cézanne's rented studio in the rue Boulegon or in his new studio in Chemin des Lauves. It has been suggested that it is a portrait of Hortense – the usual assumption when the sitter is unknown – but this is now discounted; the figure is too stylish and the volume of the head and its features resemble none of the portraits of his wife. The structure of the painting is very tightly organized and fully painted and is unusual in at least one respect; the face is depicted with a clear expression and there is an apparent search for a likeness rather than the overall structural identity so common in Cézanne's portraits. Analysis of the background is more than difficult: the forms are unidentifiable, the dark area mysterious, and the purpose of the wavy line (seemingly unrelated) is obscure. There is one feature encountered elsewhere; the table-top edge appears to be at two angles, a distortion that Cézanne frequently arrives at for the clear identification of relationships. In this painting one can discern the seeds of Cubism.

PLATE 37
Self-Portrait in Felt Hat (1890–94)
Oil on canvas, 23²/₃ x 19¹/₄ inches (60 x 49cm)

As in Peasant in a Blue Smock *(plate 34), there are small areas in this painting that are uncovered and here it is clearly not for any other reason than that Cézanne could not decide what to place there in each location. He has worked steadily on the head which is, apart from an area near the ear, completely realized. The coat is, however, unresolved; the shape of the arm is integrated but its identity is not and, since he could not resolve it, he stopped. Or if this is not so, and there is no evidence on the point, there is certainly some reason since it would have taken any other painter of the time a minute or so to have taken the uncovered areas to a finished stage. There is a different pictorial dynamic in this self-portrait from that in the previous works illustrated (plates 11 and 13). There is a sliding temporary character here, a spiky sense of movement which contrasts with the other versions. The subject is the same, recognizably, but the painting is different in pictorial not representational content. It is an explanation of Cézanne's importance.*

PLATE 38
In the Grounds of the Château Noir
(c.1899) detail
Oil on canvas, 36¼ x 28¾ inches (92 x 73cm)

When their mother died in 1897, his sister Marie took charge of settling Cézanne's affairs and under pressure from her brother-in-law Maxime Conil agreed to the sale of Jas de Bouffan. This changed the pattern of Cézanne's life, depriving him of his one settled home and the centre of his painting life. Henceforward, from 1899 until almost the end of his life, he lived unhappily, something of a displaced person in a number of different rented

accommodations. The Château Noir, halfway between Aix and Le Tholonet was where he rented a small room from which he went on painting expeditions looking for a motif within its rocky wooded grounds. In order to find a permanent location he offered to buy the château but was refused. The painting illustrated is a fine example of Cézanne's landscape style at this period in his life. The closely-knit organization of the picture area, the keen search for internal relationships and the extraordinary sense of individual identity, all characteristics of his work, are apparent here. Note the surging strength of the sapling on the left against the solid blocks of rock, each supporting the living identity of the other.

PLATE 39
The Bibémus Quarry (1898–1900)
Oil on canvas, 25½ x 21¼ inches (65 x 54cm)

Another place that Cézanne rented after the sale of Jas de Bouffan was a small cabin in the Bibémus quarry which he had rented a few years earlier while in search of his motifs. It is clear that in this painting his interest lay in the relationship between the bulbous tree shape, seeming almost like a gigantic flower, and the rock immediately below it, carrying the vertical continuation of the tree-trunk. The sense of relationship between the growing form and the immutable rock is palpable and carries echoes throughout the composition.

PLATE 40
Still-Life with Apples and Oranges (c. 1899)
Oil on canvas, 29 x 36²/₃ inches (74 x 93cm)

*Cézanne's later still-life paintings become increasingly elaborate
and sumptuous and of them all this is perhaps the most richly
conceived and painted with the greatest fluidity and assurance. All
the features of Cézanne's treatment of this subject-matter are
present. There is also an almost baroque feeling in the free
disposition of the cloth and fruit which all seem almost to float in
a frozen, flat space, emphasized by the high close angle from
which it is viewed. The changes in the angle of perspective from
front to back draws the viewer from the bottom towards the top
(this is also encountered in Degas' late bather paintings) and into
the picture space where the blank wall and decorative fabrics halt
the eye. The patterned textile, a carpet, perhaps, is the same as
the table covering in plate 36.*

PLATE 41
Portrait of Ambroise Vollard (1899)
Oil on canvas, 39½ x 32 inches (100.3 x 81.3cm)

Vollard made a number of comments in relation to this portrait in addition to the one mentioned in the introduction and they are all highly revealing of Cezanne's procedures. Cézanne's reply to another observation which Vollard made on the patches of bare canvas showing through the hands is also revealing: '…if I put something there by guesswork I might have to paint the whole canvas over again, starting from that point.' The bare patches are still there, Vollard made no further observations, and kept so quiet that he drifted into sleep and shifted his body which

prompted the famous rebuke, 'Wretch! You're changing the pose! I say to you in all truth, you must remain still like an apple. Does an apple fidget?' The composition is based on a cruciform, popular with Cézanne, the horizontal of which, on a slightly different level on either side of the head, is balanced by a clear off-vertical running from above the head through the division in the famous shirt-front, the jacket and finishing in the lower leg on the edge of the canvas. The pictorial structure suggests the first stages of the surface organization of a later Cubist composition by Picasso or Braque. The relationship between the shape of the shirt-front and Vollard's head emphasizes the significance that the shirt-front held for Cézanne in the tightly-knit composition.

Continued from page 202

individual picture identity – which has had such an important effect upon the most important of the modern pictorial developments. Put in a slightly more prosaic form, Maurice Denis' now famous dictum is appropriate here: 'Remember that a painting, before it is a horse, a nude or some sort of anecdote, is essentially a flat surface covered with colours arranged in a certain order.' For Cézanne, the consciousness of the identity of the art object (the canvas and paint) as distinct and separate was omnipresent as in itself the only pictorial reality. The finding of that unique separate identity was the core of Cézanne's struggle. This is revealed in many of his comments and observations as reported by his friends, notably Ambroise Vollard, who was also his dealer. One of the most entertaining and illuminating is Vollard's description of the painting process when Cézanne undertook his portrait. One story from the account is well known and revealing. After 115 sittings, in which Vollard was commanded to sit still like an apple: 'Apples don't move do they?' said Vollard, exhausted, but hopefully enquiring how the work was progressing. Cézanne replied, 'The front of the shirt is not bad.' That is worth thinking about. Incidentally, the portrait was never finished, the two white spots are still on the hand.

Émile Bernard, who late in Cézanne's life had many conversations with him and recorded much of what he

said, described how Cézanne was in the habit of describing with his hands the meaning he intended – for instance as follows; 'I have my *motif* [he joins his hands]. A *motif*, you see, is this [he draws his hands apart, fingers spread out, and brings them together again, slowly; then joins them, presses them together and contracts them, making them interlace]. There you have it; that is what one must attain.'

For the last 30 years of his life, that pictorial presence to enfold his *motif* was worked through in some of the most influential works in the history of Western art. His subjects were not obscure or suggestive (at least for him) of some grander intellectual message; they existed in total justification as themselves.

Cézanne's remoteness from the recognized centre of art in Paris resulted in his achievements remaining unacknowledged until the next generation, as the new century approached, began to see in this hermit-like figure, qualities that were missing from the whole repertoire of Impressionist or academic painting. From the beginning of the century, the rise in Cézanne's reputation and influence began to increase and continues.

PLATE 42
Mont Sainte-Victoire (1904–05)
Oil on canvas, 23²/₃ x 28³/₄ inches (60 x 73cm)

In November 1901, Cézanne bought some land north of Aix-en-Provence with an extensive view of the town and the surrounding countryside including, of course, Mont Sainte-Victoire. On this site on the Chemin des Lauves he built a house with a large studio and high windows, opening south onto the town with another even larger window looking north. From 1902 Cézanne worked almost full-time in the studio from which he could see the mountain and where he began a last series of paintings in oil and watercolour of this early subject. It is, of course, interesting to compare the two series from slightly different viewpoints (see also plates 21, 43 and 44). Undoubtedly the Les Lauves view is the more dramatic; it rises on a gradual slope on the north and ends in an enormous rocky peak which falls away almost vertically towards the valley plain north-east of Aix where it is peopled by farms and fields interspersed with trees and copses. The scene seemed to have held for him the oppositions which defined his emotional and physical conflicts and he succeeds (in these paintings and drawings before his most significant subject) in achieving a resolution which provides the culmination of his pictorial odyssey. The struggle reduces itself into his synthesizing of nature into art and art as nature.

In the earlier series of the 1880s, Cézanne discovers and combines the various elements of the scene in which the mountain figures in relationship with the foreground pine trees and the middle-distant valley of the Arc with the viaduct, so that it dominates, but distantly, the pastoral scene. The structured space coincides with the pictorial identity, providing the unity and harmony that at that time was his intention and struggle.

In the later series of 11 paintings and a large number of watercolour and drawn sketches, a new priority has emerged. The art, that is the canvas and its paint, is the landscape, the motif, that draws only what it needs from nature to enable it to live its own independent life. Maurice Denis, a friend who was with Cézanne in Aix for part of the time during the second series, made a watercolour study of Cézanne painting on the Les Lauves site. He was a painter and member of the Nabis group and he made a now well known observation that 'before a painting is a horse, a nude or some sort of anecdote it is essentially colours arranged on a flat surface in a certain order'. Cézanne's achievement is that he established the primacy of that order as the pictorial imperative. Much of 20th-century art depends from that achievement and, incidentally, explains the proposition offered at the beginning of the introduction to this book.

PLATE 43
Mont Sainte-Victoire from Les Lauves
(1904–05)
Oil on canvas, 23²/₃ x 28³/₄ inches (60 x 73cm)
(See caption on page 215)

PLATE 44
Mont Sainte-Victoire (1904–06)

Oil on canvas, 25 x 32²/₃ inches (63.5 x 83cm)

(*See caption on page 215*)

PLATE 45
Bathers (1902–06)
Oil on canvas, 81⅞ x 98 inches (208 x 249cm)

During the last decade of his life, Cézanne returned to a subject that he had begun to explore in the 1880s – the construction of nude figure compositions that would extend the tradition of such historical paintings into his own pictorial aesthetic. In his earlier work he had used male figures and wished to construct the new studies with female nudes. This presented him with real problems, not the least because he was nervous of women and found it difficult to contemplate approaching them to ask them to remove their clothes; at best he thought he might get 'some very old flesh' (très vieille carne, *as he put it to Vollard, whose portrait he was painting when contemplating the nudes) to undertake this indelicate activity. In the event, he did make some studies from an older model but the main source for the figures he used were the drawings he had made at the Atelier Suisse many years earlier as a student and from his memory of the female body. It might be mentioned here that although his earlier drawings are academic in intention and keenly analytical and of great interest, they are not fluently constructed. Nevertheless, the figures represented in the paintings are not the result of an incapability of representing the human form in a traditional way but essentially because he was pursuing the same pictorial solutions, at the end of his life, that had concerned him since the last of his Impressionist paintings. These great works are a further presage of the 20th-century revolution represented by Cubism and Picasso's* Demoiselles d'Avignon, *in which the images present an analysis of the subject in the form of integrated elements derived from the necessary organization of the canvas surface to make a single unit. The awkwardness that appears in the figures comes from the unification of figures and landscape into a single object – an affecting painted area.*

It will not be necessary or possible to analyse these larger works of Cézanne's late career in a few words. Or indeed any number of words for any work of art. When all that can be said has been said, every work of art can still only ultimately speak in its own language; in this case, in paint and only the examination in visual terms that is not translatable will provide the real pictorial nourishment. These last paintings are difficult but finally enormously rewarding. It has already been noted that Cézanne found it difficult finally to finish a work and none of these Bathers *is completed although he worked on them for over a decade. They demand and deserve the viewer's close attention. It will be well worth-while.*

PLATE 46
Bathers (1906)
Oil on canvas, $51\frac{1}{4}$ x $76\frac{3}{4}$ inches (130 x 195cm)
(See caption on page 221)

ACKNOWLEDGEMENT

The Publishers wish to thank the following for providing photographs, and for permission to reproduce copyright material. While every effort has been made to trace and acknowledge copyright-holders, we wish to apologize should any omissions have been made.

Paul Cézanne

Hulton Images

Still-Life with Leg of Mutton and Bread

Kunsthaus, Zurich/Giraudon, Paris

Achille Emperaire

Musée d'Orsay/Giraudon, Paris

Head of an Old Man

Musée d'Orsay/Giraudon, Paris

A Modern Olympia

Musée d'Orsay/Giraudon, Paris

Still-Life with Green Pot and Pewter Jug

Musée d'Orsay/Lauros/Giraudon, Paris

The House of the Hanged Man, Auvers

Musée d'Orsay/Giraudon, Paris

Dr. Gachet's House in Auvers

Private Collection/Giraudon, Paris

Flowers in a Delft Vase

Private Collection

Dahlias

Musée d'Orsay/Lauros/Giraudon, Paris

Self-Portrait

Pushkin Museum, Moscow/Giraudon, Paris

Three Bathers

Musée du Petit-Palais, Paris/Giraudon, Paris

Self-Portrait

Musée d'Orsay/Lauros/Giraudon, Paris

Female Nude on Sofa

Von der Heydt Museum, Wuppertal/Giraudon, Paris

The Château at Médan

Art Gallery and Museum, Glasgow/Giraudon, Paris

Still-Life with Apples and Biscuits

Musée de l'Orangerie/Lauros/Giraudon, Paris

Still-Life with Apples and Biscuits

Private Collection/Giraudon, Paris

Poplars

Musée d'Orsay/Lauros/Giraudon, Paris

The Aqueduct

Pushkin Museum, Moscow/Giraudon, Paris

Still-Life with Fruits, Napkin and Milk Jug

Musée de l'Orangerie/Lauros/Giraudon, Paris

Mont Sainte-Victoire with Large Pine

Phillips' Collection, Washington D.C./Lauros/Giraudon, Paris

The Bay of Marseille seen from L'Estaque

Musée d'Orsay/Lauros/Giraudon, Paris

Pierrot and Harlequin

Pushkin Museum, Moscow/Giraudon, Paris

The Card Players

Courtauld Institute Galleries/Bridgeman, Giraudon, Paris

Man Smoking a Pipe

Courtauld Institute Galleries/Bridgeman, Giraudon, Paris

The Smoker

Stadtische Kunsthalle, Mannheim/Giraudon, Paris

The interior and exterior of Cézanne's studio in Aix-en-Provence (photograph)

Giraudon, Paris

An elderly Cézanne in his studio working on the *Large Bathers* (photograph)

Musée Marmottan/Giraudon, Paris

Still-Life of Pot of Flowers and Pears

Courtauld Institute Galleries/Bridgeman, Giraudon, Paris

The House of Bellevue

Private Collection/Giraudon, Paris

The Great Pine

Museum of Art, Sao Paulo/Giraudon, Paris

The Lac d'Annecy

Courtauld Institute Galleries/Bridgeman, Giraudon, Paris

Still-Life with Fruit Basket (The Kitchen Table)

Musée Marmottan/Giraudon, Paris

Peasant in a Blue Smock

Christie's, London/Bridgeman/Giraudon, Paris

Portrait of Madame Cézanne

Musée de l'Orangerie/Lauros/Giraudon, Paris

Woman in Blue

The Hermitage Museum, St. Petersburg/Giraudon, Paris

Self-Portrait in Felt Hat

Bridgestone Museum of Art, Tokyo/Giraudon, Paris

In the Grounds of the Château Noir

Musée de l'Orangerie/Lauros/Giraudon, Paris

The Bibémus Quarry

Sam Spiegel Collection, New York/Lauros/Giraudon, Paris

Still-Life with Apples and Oranges

Musée d'Orsay/Lauros/Giraudon, Paris

Portrait of Ambroise Vollard

Musée du Petit-Palais, Paris/Giraudon, Paris

Mont Sainte-Victoire

Kunsthaus, Zurich/Giraudon, Paris

Mont Sainte-Victoire from Les Lauves

Courtauld Institute Galleries/Bridgeman, Giraudon, Paris

Mont Sainte-Victoire

Pushkin Museum, Moscow/Giraudon, Paris

Bathers

Philadelphia Museum of Art/Bridgeman, Giraudon, Paris

Bathers

The National Gallery, London/Bridgeman, Giraudon, Paris

Edgar Degas

Trewin Copplestone

List of Plates

The qualities which distinguish the significant creative artist from the talented amateur are not easy to establish precisely. But distinction is usually immediately recognizable, even when the subject-matter chosen by the artist is not itself especially attractive or appealing in a conventional sense. Such significant qualities are not essentially, or even primarily, technical but lie ultimately in the nature and sensitivity, the innate individuality of the artist and his ability to find an effective form in which to express them. Quality differences are unique to each individual and are part of the human condition.

It is this quality of distinctive originality that is immediately apparent in the work of Edgar Degas. Of course, it is important also to acknowledge and examine his ability to use those of the techniques available to him that effectively express his intentions. This study considers Degas' life, character and artistic achievement. Since no one lives outside his social and cultural context, the background to his life will be considered where appropriate and helpful.

The popular romantic perception of the 19th-century Parisian artist as a bohemian, given to excesses, living and working in a dingy garret in the back streets of Montmartre, was very different from the milieu into which Degas was born and grew up and which conditioned his future attitudes and behaviour. His life, at least in his earlier years, was one of quiet privilege and

PLATE 1
Self-Portrait with Crayon (1855)
Canvas and oil on paper, $31^7/_8$ x $25^1/_2$ inches
(81 x 64.5cm)

Degas' portraits of himself bear out his determination to be a realist – which is what he had wished the name of the first exhibition of the Independent group to reflect. This painting is an unequivocal image of a self-satisfied, self-indulgent young man, lacking humour. But however convincingly he misrepresents himself (since he had a strong sense of humour, and was witty and hard-working), the pursed mouth suggests a supercilious nature that events later confirmed. As a portrait, it is brilliant, uncompromising and, as he himself wished it to be – honest. He is holding a drawing crayon which indicates an interest which at that time and despite his father's disapproval, was beginning to dominate his hopes for a future career. The quality of the draughtsmanship in so young a man, not yet 21, is astonishingly precise, sensitive and assured. He painted most of his self-portraits before he reached the age of 25.

PLATE 2
René-Hilaire De Gas (1857)
Oil on canvas, 20⁷/₈ x 16 inches (53 x 41cm)

This portrait of Degas' grandfather was the result of a visit to Naples in 1856. He made a number of studies and drawings while there, and his grandfather's forbidding appearance is clearly delineated. It is likely that as his oldest grandson Degas would have been particularly cherished and despite the sour patrician look, the portrait indicates that Degas was afforded a great deal of time in order to study his grandfather. It is

perhaps not unexpected that with his noble ancestry, René-Hilaire was unsympathetic to the Revolution, and two events must have reinforced his views. Firstly, his fiancée was guillotined after showing friendship to the Prussians and, if the story is true, he himself received a warning when he displayed sympathy for Marie Antoinette at her execution. In the event, he left France, went to Egypt and after an adventurous if sparsely documented period, settled in Naples, becoming first a corn merchant then subsequently founding the bank which became the source of the financial security that Degas enjoyed in his early years.

financial security. He had no need to follow a career and becoming a painter was born out of an intellectual passion for a cultured, creative life. Not for him the driven torment of Van Gogh or the romantic quest of Gauguin; indeed, on one occasion when asked whether he painted out-of-doors, *en plein-air*, he is reported as replying, 'Why would I, painting is not a sport.' Later in life he put this view more pungently: 'You know what I think of painters who work in the open. If I were the government I would have a company of gendarmes watching out for men who paint landscapes from nature. Oh, I don't wish for anybody's death; I should be quite content with a little bird-shot to begin with ...Renoir, that's different he can do what he likes.'

Hilaire-Germain-Edgar Degas was born on 19 July 1834 at 8 rue Saint-Georges, Paris, the son of the manager of the Paris branch of the private family bank owned by his grandfather, who then lived in Naples. His father was a cultured man with a passionate interest in the arts who had a considerable influence over his son's early development. His mother, Célestine Musson, was of Creole origin and came from New Orleans. (The Creoles of Louisiana were the French, Spanish or Portuguese descendants of settlers who retained their own patois and culture.) Although she died when Edgar was a child, the family retained its links with the town and Degas, late in 1872, went there for an extended visit which resulted in one of his most important

early works, a painting somewhat out of context with his usual subject-matter, *The Cotton Exchange at New Orleans* (plate 15).

Degas was always a proud, reserved individual, something of a misogynist, conscious of his social status and with a sharp, witty tongue and cool temperament. His whole demeanour and background seemed to preclude an artistic career and his father, while encouraging his son's interest in the intellectual life of the capital saw him, in the true sense, as an amateur, that is to say a 'lover', of the arts, and was hardly sympathetic when he learnt of his son's wish to dedicate himself to painting. Of course, there was no financial necessity for Degas to sell his paintings and, like many artists, he had a distaste for commerce. He could not even bear to be parted from his works and clients buying his paintings quickly became aware of his habit of asking for them back in order that he could add some 'finishing touches', after which he sometimes failed to return the paintings to their owners. Most clients, growing wise to the practice, usually succeeded in recapturing their property on a subsequent visit; but there were many times when sharp words ensued, and there is at least one occasion of a painting never being returned. In his early 20s, Degas had so far identified himself in his comment: 'It seems to me that today, if the artist wishes to be serious ... he must once more sink himself into solitude.' Through

Continued on page 240

PLATE 3
The Bellelli Family (c.1858–60)
Oil on canvas, 78³/₄ x 98³/₈ inches (200 x 250cm)

Degas was very fond of his aunt Laura, his father's sister, and after leaving Rome was invited to visit her in Florence where she lived with her husband, Baron Gennaro Bellelli and their daughters, Giovanna and Giulia. It was Degas' original intention to paint his aunt and her daughters, but the painting eventually included Baron Bellelli, a decision which caused his father some concern since Gennaro was an unpredictable character. It was constructed from a number of separate sketches and completed in Paris. Degas' first composition was not entirely satisfactory to him and he returned to Florence to make more studies, including a full sketch of the intended composition. Back in Paris he completed the revised working during 1860. There are a number of unresolved questions posed by the painting, not the least being the identity of the significant, defining rectangular portrait in the background. Laura is wearing black as her father René-Hilaire had recently died and it is suggested that the work was intended as a memento mori. *Another suggestion is that the background picture is of her brother Auguste, Degas' father, and a different interpretation is possible if this is true. However, the composition does break new ground in that it is an interpretation in modern terms of the familiar Renaissance family portraits which Degas much admired.*

PLATE 4
Semiramis Founding Babylon (1861) detail
Oil on canvas, 59³/₈ x 101¹/₂ inches (151 x 258cm)

Under the influence of Ingres and the academic tradition of historical or mythological paintings, Degas made a number of paintings or sketches for such subjects in the early years of his development. The mythological Assyrian queen, Semiramis, the wife of Nunus founder of Ninevah, was the most powerful figure in the early stories of the building of the Assyrian empire, including the whole construction of Babylon, the road system, the conquests of Egypt, Ethiopia and Libya, and numerous other feats. She was also a goddess, the daughter of the Syrian goddess Derketo. She is Rossini's Semiramide and for some time it was believed that Degas drew inspiration from this source since it was performed at the Paris Opéra in 1860 and Degas was an opera fan: this source of the painting is, however, now discounted. In the academic terms then dominant, the painting is an attractive and delicate example, constructed with great restraint. There is a study drawing of the horse which shows the extraordinary distinction of Degas' draughtsmanship, even at this early stage of his career.

Continued from page 234

his life he was a solitary and towards the end was almost a recluse. (It is interesting to note that William Morris, the leader of the Arts and Crafts movement in England, was born in March of the same year as Degas.)

In 1845, at the age of 12, Degas entered the Lycée Louis le Grand as a boarder where he received a full classical education which naturally included the study of Greek and Latin. The lycée had a considerable influence on him: while there, he developed his life-long passion for the French classics, in particular the works of Racine, Pascal, La Rochefoucauld, Gautier and Flaubert, which, together with his classical training, fed his maturing intellect and complemented his original, questing spirit. His schooldays had another important effect on his later life in that while at the lycée he formed friendships with a number of his fellows which continued for the remainder of their respective lives. Notable among these were Henri Rouart and Paul Valpinçon, both of whom figured importantly in his later life.

In 1853, and in deference to his father's opposition to his becoming an artist, Degas entered law school although, once there, his lack of concern for his studies and his expanding interest in the arts were so compelling that he spent most of his time drawing, visiting the studios of artist acquaintances and the private collections of his friends while also studying for many hours in the galleries

PLATE 5

Scene of War in the Middle Ages 1865

(also known as ***Les Malheurs de la Ville d'Orléans***)
Oil on paper, mounted on canvas, 33¹/₂ x 57⁷/₈ inches
(85 x 147cm)

When one recalls Degas' devotion to 'realism', this painting is somewhat baffling. It might be remembered that Manet exhibited his painting, Olympia, *which caused a scandal since it depicted a nude and suggested to viewers through its evident realism what*

critics took to be proof that she was a prostitute. In this painting, included in the Salon of 1865, there are several nudes, realistically depicted with overtones of sexual violence. It will also be noticed that one of the executioners, herself a woman, is in the act of killing another woman in a way which looks very like sport to her. On the right there is part of the figure of a naked woman being abducted and there is undoubtedly a salacious content to the work. It is therefore reasonable to ask why this painting appears to have caused no offence? There is, too, some difficulty in interpreting the intention or subject. Until recently, the association

with Orléans was part of the title but no such event took place during the Middle Ages as far as is known. Of course, there may have been some association in Degas' mind with New Orleans, the American city from which his mother originated, but what this might have been is not known. This was the last of Degas' history paintings and it is interesting to note that he signed the picture bottom right, Ed. De Gas, his actual family name. The scandal caused by Manet's picture, Le déjeuner sur l'herbe, is considered on page 255.

PLATE 6
Self-Portrait with Hat (1862)
Oil on canvas, 19 x 24$^{1}/_{4}$ inches (48.5 x 61.5cm)

Although recognizably the same person portrayed in the self-portrait painted six or seven years earlier (plate 1), there is a supercilious assurance in the demeanour of the Degas of the later work. A comparison will indicate a subtle significant change in the eye-level used in the straightforward gaze on equal terms with the viewer in the earlier work to the slightly downward enquiring glance of the later – a slight but unmistakable reflection of a new awareness or assumption of his own superiority. One searches in vain in this picture for the Degas described by his peers as witty, charming and companionable. Could it perhaps then be a revelation of an underlying insecurity? The drawing of the hand and glove, acutely observed and carefully delineated, clearly reveals the influence of Ingres at the early stage of his career.

of the Louvre. He also enrolled in the print-room of the Bibliothèque Nationale where he made copies of great Renaissance masters such as Mantegna, Leonardo and Holbein. It was his habit to keep notebooks of his reactions and observations and in one from this period observed: 'Seek to blend the spirit of Mantegna's armour with the animation and colour of Veronese' – a prescient comment on the nature of his achievement; fine drawing with refined colour. Yet another: 'Painting is the art of surrounding a spot of Venetian red in such a way that it appears vermilion.' For Degas, the sum of these experiences of Renaissance art was to confirm a devotion to the classical spirit to which he had been introduced in early childhood and to reinforce an admiration for the Renaissance form of linear draughtsmanship which distinguished his work.

It was during this time, in the collection of Paul Valpinçon's father, that Degas first saw a number of works by Jean-Auguste-Dominique Ingres, recognized as the great academic successor of the Neo-Classicist Jacques-Louis David and himself acknowledged as a fine draughtsman. Soon afterwards Degas met Ingres and developed a reverence and admiration for the man then regarded as the greatest painter of the time, feelings which remained with him for the rest of his life; he never forgot Ingres'advice: '...draw lines, young man, draw lines; whether from memory or after nature. Then you will be a good artist.'

At the age of 21 Degas entered the studio of Louis Lamothe, a former student of Ingres; but the association was not a very happy or fruitful one. He finishes a letter to Gustave Moreau with the observation, 'Lamothe is more foolish than ever'. More profitably, he also studied at the École des Beaux Arts where he met other young and eager painters, including Léon Bonnat and Fantin-Latour, both later to become, with Degas, well known independent painters. It was at this stage that Degas began to acquire those qualities of draughtsmanship which are revealed for the first time in the many drawings he made of himself and his family. It should be remembered that during most of the 19th century, the normal method of study was to enter the studio of a recognized painter/master as an apprentice so that his period with Lamothe is nevertheless his first professional step.

Degas made his first of a number of visits to Italy in 1857, ostensibly to visit his grandfather in Naples and his aunt (his father's sister was married to a Baron Bellelli), but was perhaps as much drawn to the classical Latin culture that he knew he would encounter in Italy. In fact, from 1857 to 1860 he spent much of each year in Rome where a number of his old friends were then living and through whom he made a number of new friends. His deep interest in music was encouraged by his meeting there with Georges Bizet who was four years his junior and who had won the first Prix de Rome in 1857. Significantly, the most important meeting Degas made in Rome was with

PLATE 7
Gentleman's Race: Before the Start (1862)
Oil on canvas, 19 x 24¼ inches (48.5 x 61.5cm)

Degas made the first studies of horses and racing subjects in 1861 and during the 1860s produced a number of studies and paintings of this 'sport of gentlemen' which, for Degas, was an appropriate interest for one of his level in society. Not surprisingly, these subjects were popular and their appearance signalled the end of his academic paintings without affecting the character or quality of his draughtsmanship. The title of this painting will indicate the riders' amateur status and the crowd in the middle-distance is clearly 'society'. Just to emphasize the point, perhaps, Degas has included the smoke stacks of industry − where the workers are! His interest in racing subjects was replaced by other concerns but his interest in horses remained and appears later in his work. (See also plates 8 and 9.)

Gustave Moreau who was there on a visit from Paris. Moreau was a painter raised in the academic tradition who favoured large biblical or classical subjects, treated with great attention to detail. He was highly intelligent and sophisticated and was recognized as an inspirational teacher. Temperamentally a Romantic symbolist with a highly developed sense of the mystical, through his widely ranging knowledge he introduced Degas to the Venetian Renaissance colourists, especially Titian. Moreau had also been working with Chassériau, a pupil of Delacroix, and through him directed Degas to the work of Delacroix, that painterly and colourful Romantic who in his early days had been an independent and had achieved a fame outside the Salon comparable to that of Ingres. Therefore, before 1860, Degas had been introduced to the work of the greatest painters of both the Classical and Romantic traditions, Ingres and Delacroix, and had absorbed much inspiration and food for thought from these two disparate but important figures.

Moreau, it is also significant to note, was a pastellist whose intense, brilliant colour had considerable effect on Degas' own unique use of the method, and in which he produced many of his finest works − particularly in his later years. It would not be an exaggeration to say that Degas was himself one of the finest of all pastellists.

During 1858 Degas made a long visit to his aunt in

Continued on page 251

PLATE 8
At the Racecourse, with Jockeys in Front of the Stands (1869–72)
Essence on canvas, 18¹/₈ x 24 inches (46 x 61cm)

Degas and Manet, as befitted their upper middle-class image, frequented the races and both made paintings of racing subjects. For Manet it was the movement and bustle of the crowds and the speeding horses that interested him; for Degas it was the parade or the period before the race began. His images are clear and the drawing acutely observed. His unusual sense of colour and liking for sharp contrasts and highlights were especially catered for in the subject and most of his paintings offer unexpected compositional qualities. This painting, in essence not oil, is a study for a larger work and is lightly and thinly painted on a toned canvas. The running horse in the distance indicates that he had not yet seen the Muybridge photographs of horses running.

Degas used essence as a sketching medium since he wanted the effect of oil without the long drying time, and was easy to handle. Essence is the term used to identify a dried oil mixed with a volatile spirit, probably turpentine.

PLATE 9

Amateur Jockeys on the Course, beside an Open Carriage (c.1877)

Oil on canvas, 26 x 31⁷/₈ inches (66 x 81cm)

Degas' interest in racing subjects had declined by the mid 1870s but this accomplished painting with its bold compositional devices shows that he continued to find many aspects of the races attractive. This work, emphasizing the aura of privilege which surrounded much of 19th-century racing, reveals that the amateur jockeys themselves are part of the same social stratum as the carriage owners and are here seen hobnobbing with the ladies before the race. The composition is almost that of a photograph, a snap-shot image, since the focus of interest of the observer, the 'photographer', is concentrated on the jockey who looks to the left (at a friend?) and this results in the carriage being only partly seen, the main space in the frame being landscape. The naturalness of this compositional effect is characteristic of Degas and represents his real interest in photography.

PLATE 10
Léon Bonnat (c. 1863)
Oil on canvas, 17 x 14⅛ (43 x 36cm)

It is probable that Degas met Léon Bonnat, who was one year older, at the École des Beaux Arts in Paris in 1855 and they certainly met in 1858 in Rome. Bonnat won the second Grand Prix de Rome and it was there that he met Degas

who was one of a small group he joined. Bonnat later became a fashionable portrait-painter and a museum was created in his name in his native city of Bayonne after his death in 1922. Degas described him as 'nice and an old friend', although he did not greatly admire his painting. Bonnat was one of those friends that Degas painted while he was still an amateur and not receiving commissions or using professional models.

Continued from page 245

Florence. Here he made numerous studies of members of the family – notably his two young female cousins – and used them on his return to Paris to produce his first group portrait in oils (plate 3). This effectively determined his own private, personal and professional attachment to art. Of his feelings and character, his own travel notes are often revealing. 'I am now going back to the life of Paris. Who knows what will happen? But I shall always be an honest man.'

This return happily coincided with the new influences becoming apparent in Degas' work. He became aware of Japanese prints which were then beginning to appear in France after the opening of trade with Japan in 1854. These were sometimes used to wrap small imported objects. Degas was a friend of Félix Braquemond, an engraver, who in 1856 had discovered the prints of Hokusai and introduced Degas to his work. Japonaiserie became the vogue in France during the 1860s, later popularized by the Oriental Pavilions in the Universal Exhibitions of 1867 and 1878. Many artists, particularly those outside the restrictive academic world, were attracted to aspects of oriental art. Whistler was perhaps the most enthusiastic follower of the fashion, but Monet discovered a clarity in the prints and Manet recognized the strong tension existing between light and dark oppositions. Both incorporated something of these elements in their own

work, without becoming overtly orientalist. Degas, on whom the influence was possibly the most subtle, was impressed by the compositional qualities that seemed innovational – figures non-centralized, asymmetrical and foreshortened as well as figures cut by the borders and brought close to picture plane to create an intimate direct association. Their unfamiliar character and composition, offering a new and original visual imagery, had a considerable impact on many artists in the middle and late years of the 19th century and for Degas had a positive effect on his compositional methods.

Perhaps even more significant for Degas was the advent of photography. A number of painters saw it as a threat to their exclusive ability in the field of visual representation which was, for many, the principal or only artistic justification. One well known painter, Paul Delaroche, is recorded as commenting on sight of his first photograph, 'From today painting is dead'. For Degas, however, it was both an aid and an inspiration. He saw photography as providing visual information not readily available (particularly in respect of human and animal movement) as well as, in 'snapshot' views, offering original compositional solutions (see plate 9). In later life, Degas' interest became a passion at least partly inspired by his seriously deteriorating eyesight, photographs providing a record of a model or other subject from a necessary distance that he would otherwise have been unable to capture. There is a story of

PLATE 11
Thérèse De Gas (c. 1863)
Oil on canvas, 35 x 26¹⁄₃ inches (89 x 67cm)

Thérèse was Degas' sister and eight years his junior. She married Edmondo Morbilli, her cousin and a member of a noble Italian family (he was Duke of Morbilli), in 1863. During the early period of his career, before the failure of the family bank, Degas painted a number of portraits of family and friends since he was

not at that time a 'professional' painter. (That is only to explain that he did not then make a living from painting and is not a comment on the quality of his work.) He painted these portraits to further his own experience. However, the distinction of the paintings was attractive to all his sitters. One quality always present in his work is an individual sense of colour and the use of the sharp pink ribbon bow is a good example of its heightening effect on the whole painting. It may be noted that the painting has suffered some damage.

his leaving a dinner-table to fetch his camera so that he could pose all the guests for a composition to be completed later.

A CHANGING WORLD: ROMANTICISM AND REALISM

Degas became involved with the Parisian art scene during a period of profound change. The French artists of the establishment, the academicians, the students in their ateliers and the artistic *haut monde* relied for their authority and standards on the accepted masters of the day and their work as displayed in the annual Salon, held in the Grand Salon of the Louvre Palace. The recognized great master of the day was Jean-Auguste-Dominique Ingres, inheritor of the mantle of Jacques-Louis David – Neo-Classicism – which, as its name implies, looked back to classical Greece and Rome (particularly Rome) for both subject-matter and style. It inspired a careful evocation of Roman architecture and, in painting, a hard precise delineation of form as well as the use of classical sources for its subject-matter. For the first half of the 19th century, it was the basis of all academically acceptable painting and was the form adopted in most painting submitted to the Salon each year.

Early in the century, though not yet acceptable, an alternative was gestating. The English poets, Shelley and Byron, were looking to other, more imaginative and less

timeworn sources, and in French painting a new and opposing reputation was coming to be recognized in the work of Eugène Delacroix, paralleled in England with that of John Constable and J. M. W. Turner. By the time that Degas was beginning to be a serious painter, this whole Romantic development had already engaged the interest of a number of young painters for whom the whole classical establishment was genuinely distasteful. Their somewhat reluctant leader was the painter Manet, and their rendezvous was the Café Guerbois in Montmartre, Paris.

Degas' probable first meeting with Édouard Manet occurred in about 1860. Manet came from the same social background as Degas and had become a painter with the hope and expectation of academic success and public recognition, at the very least rewarded with the Légion d'Honneur. But his independent nature had led him, despite his aspirations to success in the Salon, to explore a range of subject-matter and technique which, by the early 1860s, had led to his involvement with the avant garde, anti-academic group which joined him at his favourite 'waterhole', the Café Guerbois. This was partly the result of the *succès de scandale* Manet had achieved in 1863 from an unexpected and surprising source.

Beginning in 1833, a major artistic event of the Parisian social calendar was the Paris Salon which it was intended should be held every year in the Grand Salon of the Louvre (hence its name). It was opened in 1863 by

PLATE 12
Interior Scene, known as The Rape
(c. 1874 or 1868–69) detail
Oil on canvas, 31⅞ x 44⅞ inches (81 x 114cm)

A number of literary sources have been suggested as the origin of this picture. In the late 1860s and throughout the 1870s, Degas painted a number of genre works of a domestic kind, often taken from the works of contemporaries like Zola and his friend Duranty. No source has been definitely established although Zola's Madeleine Ferat seems a strong candidate. The

composition is unusual and effective. Bearing in mind the tendency to read from left to right, the fact that the girl is not dressed for a social occasion is the first element observed and the eye then swings across an open space of pretty wallpaper and a bed to the reason why she crouches, unhappy and seemingly unaware of the man looking at her with careless disregard. It is an illustration and a story well told but not one of the typically Degas paintings. It was accidentally damaged and had to be repaired and retouched by Degas with the help of a painter friend in the early 20th century when Degas' sight had seriously deteriorated.

PLATE 12 — 254 —

Napoleon III who suggested that to emphasize the superior quality of the pictures that had already been selected, those rejected by the judges should be shown in other unused galleries of the Louvre to be known as the Salon des Refusés. Although a number of independents, including future Impressionists Monet and Pissarro had been accepted for the Salon, Manet's painting, *Le déjeuner sur l'herbe* (Picnic in the Park might be a possible translation) was rejected and hung with the *refusés*. It was greeted with a barrage of hostility: Napoleon III, on opening the exhibition was said to have insisted that his wife avert her eyes from the picture. The experiment was not repeated, although similar unofficial Salons were organized in future years. Manet, admittedly somewhat obliquely, was following advice he had received from Courbet and Baudelaire to produce a painting of modern life. *Déjeuner* depicts two stylishly dressed gentlemen reclining on the grass accompanied by a naked female who looks nonchalantly and with idle curiosity directly out of the picture at the viewer, thereby establishing the voyeuristic involvement of every observer of the somewhat risqué scene. In the background of the painting another female figure is seen in a state of 'sweet disorder of the dress'. It was Manet's attempt to translate a composition from Raphael made into an engraving by Marcantonio Raimondi which, it is believed, Manet had previously seen. It was certainly a far cry from the original and although the poses of the figures were similar to those in the engraving, it was a scandalous interpretation which genuinely shocked its viewers. When Manet repeated the offence two years later with his painting of a reclining nude, *Olympia*, which also boldly and invitingly engaged the viewer's attention and which was somewhat surprisingly accepted by the Salon, he became the leader of the anti-academic independent painters who were

Continued on page 261

PLATE 13

**The Orchestra of the Opéra,
Rue Le Peletier** (1868–69)

Oil on canvas, 22¼ x 18⅛ inches (56.5 x 46.2cm)

Visitors to Paris during this century will think of the great building by Charles Garnier as the home of Parisian opera in the Place de l'Opéra, or would have done until the new Opéra Bastille was built and the other became the Opéra Garnier. But the opera house that Degas depicted in most of his paintings of the ballet was the much earlier building in the rue Le Peletier, destroyed by fire in 1873. Garnier's building, begun in 1861 was not completed until 1875. The Opéra Peletier was very convenient for Degas who lived nearby and usually visited the Opéra at least three times a week in his early and middle years. His painting of the orchestra which contains portraits of known musicians and includes the composer Chabrier (far left in the stage box), was his attempt at a group portrait and to make a decorative arrangement of musical intruments. In 1870, Degas gave the painting to the bassoonist Désiré Dihau (the central

figure) in gratitude for Dihau's introducing him to the world of the orchestra; Degas' family, in a roundabout way, also expressed their gratitude to Dihau since by keeping the painting away from Edgar, a finished work was achieved – Degas always felt that more could be done to any painting.

PLATE 14

Jeantaud, Linet and Lainé (1871)

Oil on canvas, 15 x 18⅛ inches (38 x 46cm)

Jeantaud, Linet and Lainé were friends of Degas who also served with him in a battery of the National Guard commanded by Henri Rouart during the Siege of Paris.

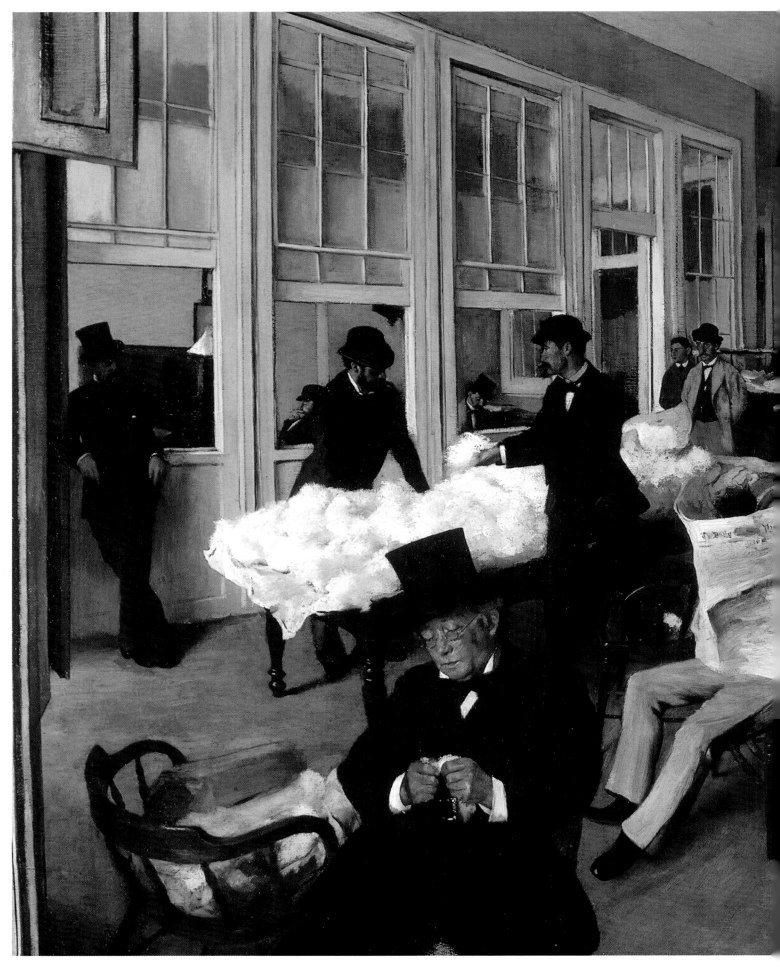

PLATE 15
The Cotton Exchange at New Orleans
(1873)
Oil on canvas, 28 x 36¼ inches (71 x 92cm)

In 1872 Degas made a visit to New Orleans and to René, his brother, who was a cotton merchant in partnership with another brother, Achille, and which gave him an opportunity to meet other members of his family. During the visit he also made studies for this painting which he finished on his return to Paris in 1873. René appears in the picture, reading a local newspaper, the Times Picayune *– possibly an indication of Degas' view of his brother's lack of industry before René's financial difficulties had emerged. Another member of the family, René's father-in-law, Michel Musson, appears as the old gentleman testing samples in the foreground. Achille, equally uninvolved in work, is seen leaning on the window on the left. The painting is another example of the* genre *paintings that Degas was producing in the 1870s, including* The Pedicure *(plate 16).*

One of Degas' devices, influenced by his photography, is to introduce a steep perspective in the foreground, thus accomplishing two effects – involvement of the viewer and at the same time identifying a deep recession. The casual atmosphere is deceptive: the oppositions of black and white are carefully distributed over the picture plane and balanced by cool green and warm ochre. The painting was sold to the museum at Pau in 1878, one of the first works of Degas to appear in a museum.

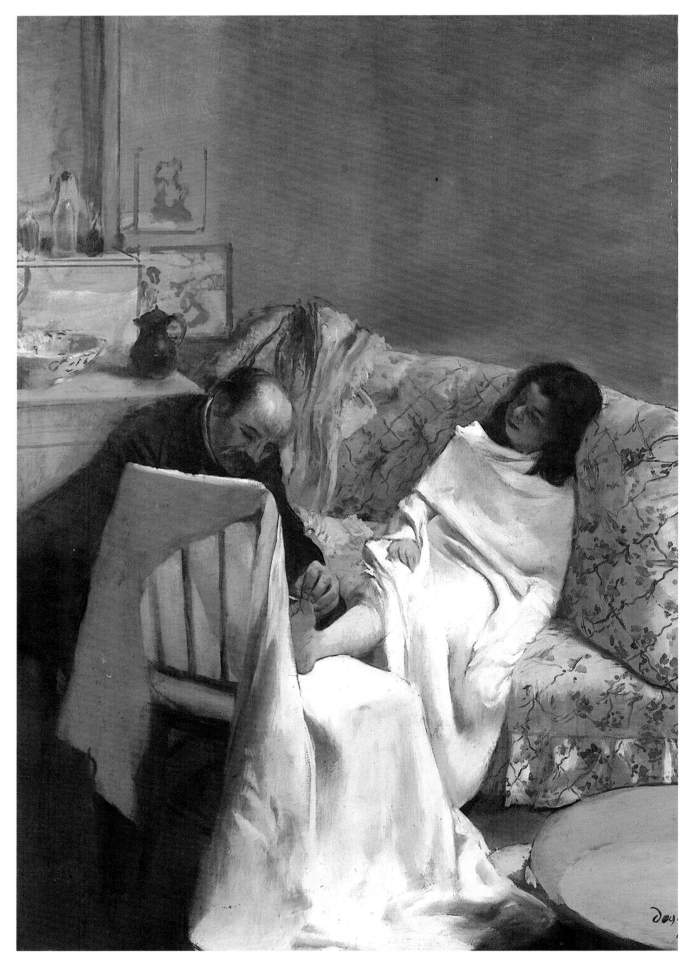

PLATE 16
The Pedicure (1873) detail
Oil on paper mounted on canvas, 24 x 18⅛ inches
(61 x 46cm)

An unusual subject in the Degas oeuvre, this was painted after his return from the visit to New Orleans from sketches made while he was there. It is suggested that the model was probably

Joe Balfour or Bell, his brother René's stepdaughter by Estelle Musson whose first husband had been killed in the American Civil War. It is an example of an approach to subject-matter that was developing in Degas' work; an unusual and intimate angle seized at a crucial moment and seen at its fullest much later in the intimate Bathers series (see plates 35–38). It was one of the paintings taken by the Louvre Gallery from the Camondo legacy.

Continued from page 255

dismayed by the predominating and, as they thought, irrelevant historicism of most of the work of the Salon.

By 1865, Degas had become Manet's friend and a participant in Café Guerbois society which included Zola, Renoir, Monet and the critic Edmond Duranty (plate 29) who became Degas' friend, admirer and promoter. Although Degas, with his classical education and devotion to Ingres (who was still alive) was not in sympathy with much of their thinking, his association with these independents nevertheless links him to the beginning of what later became the Impressionist revolution. It is important at this point to consider what this was and what part Degas played in its formation and development.

The main complaint that both of Manet's paintings had provoked arose from the fact that the starkness of the nudity had been unrelieved by the usual associated classical trappings. The effect had been to introduce a new and disturbing realism into the rarefied and privileged world of art which was then the almost exclusive preserve of the so-called intellectuals, the rich and the aristocratic. The eroticism now discernible in much 19th-century academic work was to the artistic world of the mid 19th century (particularly in France and England) merely the proper form of expression of the classically-inspired subject-matter. The fact that Manet had actually reinterpreted Renaissance subjects in a modern context had not been

recognized and even if it had been, his translation from the historical to the present would almost certainly still have resulted in his work being rejected by the establishment. On the other hand, the attention of young, questioning painters was directed to portraying modern subjects although, at this time, in traditional tonal painting techniques.

There were a number of precedents for this change. While classical themes were the most evident elements in the work of Ingres who painted a number of works that show a marked Romanticism (for example, interiors of Turkish harems), it is probable that only his loyalty to his master J.-L. David prevented his further exploration of exotic themes. His Romantic counterpart, Delacroix, had no such inhibitions and had travelled in North Africa, making sketches of Arab subjects which he translated into large compositions. These works, and those of other Romantics such as Géricault, with his painting *The Raft of the Medusa* – a naval scandal – had by the 1860s introduced a new atmosphere of freedom and experiment as well as non-historical subject-matter. There was a new realism also evident in the works of Courbet, the Barbizon painters who worked near the Forest of Fontainebleau, Boudin and the Dutch landscapist Jongkind.

However, it was soon realized by Manet's followers that he was also pursuing a new method of painting, a more appropriate technique, more modern. It was directed

PLATE 17
The Dancing Class (c. 1874) detail
Oil on canvas, 33½ x 29½ inches (85 x 75cm)

Precise dating of many of Degas' paintings is difficult since most were made from sketches made at the time of the event and then subsequently incorporated in the final work. In the ballet works during the early 1870s, it is important to remember that the performances or locations are identified as at the Opéra. As mentioned earlier, the old Opéra was in the rue Le Peletier and was burnt down in 1873; the new Garnier Opéra did not open until 1875. It is probable that this painting was executed during 1874 after the fire, but before the Garnier. It is, however, depicted as being in the Peletier Opéra where the rehearsal rooms

were in the elaborate style illustrated here. There is a very similar composition, including the dancing master in the same pose, which was painted in 1876 and located in the Garnier Opéra where the architecture in the rehearsal rooms was rather simpler.

Degas did a number of drawings and paintings of the dancers portrayed in their different poses. The dancing master, Jules Perrot, once Taglioni's partner as dancer and later a competent choreographer, was a well regarded teacher. This work is one of Degas' finest treatments of the subject and he handles the composition with his usual ingenuity and authority. Characteristic of his treatment of the dancers is the use of brightly coloured sashes, used here to great effect. Note again the steep perspective and the light touches of the small dog and watering can in the foreground.

towards finding a method of projecting a more immediate sense of actuality without 'factual' copying. It could be said, although at this time it was not, that their aim was to create a calculated 'impression' of a scene or other subject.

At all events, these young 'independent' painters in 1874 organized an exhibition which opened on 15 April at the former studio of the great early photographer Nadar and called it the 'Première Exposition de la Société Anonyme des Artistes, Peintres, Sculpteurs, Graveurs'. Degas was prominent among the organizers and exhibited with Monet and Renoir and other potential Impressionists. Among the exhibits was a painting by Monet called *Impression: Sunrise,* the title being immediately borrowed by the critic Louis Le Roy as a heading for his review, 'Exhibition of the Impressionists'. This resulted in the perpetuation of the name used to identify these young painters. Degas himself disliked the title, preferring the word independent although he would have approved of the use of 'realist'. He never described himself as an Impressionist.

Degas' career during the later 1860s consisted of work submitted to the Salon, sometimes accepted but more frequently rejected, so that in 1870 he gave up altogether. In 1865, in the same Salon as Manet's *Olympia,* he showed *Scene of War in the Middle Ages* (plate 5), a typically academic and historicist work influenced by Ingres and part of his then current programme of historical paintings

which he abandoned the next year. His painting *The Wounded Jockey,* in the 1866 Salon, indicated a new interest in horses and racing and two years later he exhibited a painting *Mlle. Fiocre in the Ballet La Source,* the first evidence of his growing passion for the theatre and ballet.

The Franco-Prussian War of 1870 was the beginning of a dramatic disruption of the cultural life of Paris and to the dispersal of writers and artists in response to war conditions. Characteristically, Degas and Manet remained in the city, joined the National Guard, and played a part in the Siege of Paris; Degas in a gun battery which, to his delight, included his two boyhood friends, Paul Valpinçon and Henri Rouart, who was the battery commander. However, as a result of exposure to cold weather while in the gun emplacements, Degas developed an eye condition which worsened steadily and affected him for the rest of his life, leading eventually to near-blindness.

As already mentioned, in 1872 Degas made a visit to New Orleans to his brother, René, a cotton merchant. He stayed from October to April the following year, during which time he made many family studies and from which, on his return to Paris, he painted his famous *Cotton Exchange at New Orleans* (plate 15). On his return, he moved to a new studio at 77 rue Blanche, frequented the Opéra, and met his friends at their new meeting-place, Café de la Nouvelle-Athènes, where they were joined by the painter Forain and the Irish writer, art observer and

PLATE 18
Dancers Resting (1874)
Oil on canvas, 33½ x 29½ inches (85 x 75cm)

Degas spent much of his time either in the wings of the theatre or in the rehearsal rooms, making studies in charcoal, crayon or pastel of dancers working or at rest and repeated the poses in

different paintings which, incidentally, was the common academic practice; a critically approved pose in a Salon work would be repeated in the next Salon submission. Both the poses shown in this painting are repeated in other works; indeed, the girl scratching her back appears in the previous plate sitting on the same piano.

critic, George Moore, whose perceptive remarks on his painter contemporaries provide us with some of the most evocative word portraits that exist. Moore describes the scene at the Nouvelle-Athènes: Manet '...sits next to Degas, that round-shouldered man in a suit of pepper and salt. There is nothing very trenchantly French about him either, except the large necktie; his eyes are small, and his words are sharp, ironical, cynical.'

In December 1873, Degas visited his father who was seriously ill in Turin and who in February of the following year died in Naples. His father's death revealed that the bank he controlled was in considerable financial difficulties and Degas as the eldest son felt a responsibility to take charge of the disturbing, near-disastrous situation. When he appealed to his brother René for help, he discovered that René was himself in difficulties and also needed financial assistance. Degas' secure life was at an end: to help settle the debts he was obliged to sell most of his important and valuable collection of paintings, including some fine pastels by Quentin La Tour, one of the greatest pastellists of the 18th century.

Not unexpectedly, this disaster changed the whole pattern of Degas' life. In Renoir's view: ' ...if Degas had died at fifty he would have been remembered as an excellent painter, no more: it is after his fiftieth year that his work broadened out and that he really became Degas.' From now on he would have to abandon his former

somewhat dilettantish existence and work as a professional painter, depending on the sale of his work for an income. It is hardly surprising that he found this an uncomfortable and depressing prospect. It should be remembered that commercial galleries and professional picture-dealers did not then exist as they do now, and the painter was obliged to sell his own work, either from his studio or from a private room. Degas' reserved nature and lingering pride in his superior social status rendered him so self-conscious, distressed and awkward with his customers that relationships with them, and even with his friends, often became acrimonious. He was also suffering increasingly from eye trouble which did little to improve his temper; many believed that, as is commonly the case, he often exaggerated his disability.

It was a time of great difficulty. While Degas' financial affairs took up most of his time, he still managed to be one of the prime movers, with Monet, in setting up the first Impressionist exhibition in 1874. This was the beginning of an interrupted series of eight exhibitions organized by the group, but known by different names. A second Impressionist exhibition took place in 1876, with the last in 1886, and Degas exhibited in all but two of them.

It is clear from this that Degas was closely associated with the development of what we now call Impressionism and it is certainly a common perception that Degas was an Impressionist. It is important in any assessment of his art to

PLATE 19
L'Absinthe (1876)
Oil on canvas, 36¼ x 26¾ inches (92 x 68cm)

For this famous work, Degas used two of his friends as models. The delightful actress Ellen Andrée and the engraver Marcellin Desboutin are seated in the Nouvelle-Athènes café in the Place Pigalle, by this time the meeting place of the independents who had already held their first Impressionist exhibition. The composition, a constructed realist work, creates an atmosphere that must have been very familiar in the cafés around the city, and quiet drinking, comfortable relationships, self-absorption or drunken oblivion were all part of the ambience. But it is important to realize that the sitters are posed and it would be unfair to assume that either Desboutin or Andrée were addicts. The placing of the figures in the top right and the sharp foreground angles leading to the two heads is a characteristically individualist Degas composition. It might be noticed that the shapes of the table-tops are not supported by legs – a visual inaccuracy but preventing a distraction. The painting was purchased by a Captain Hill of Brighton where it was exhibited in 1876, occasioning a critical comment: 'The very disgusting novelty of the subject arrests attention.'

determine to what, if any extent this perception is accurate. In these days when any perceived association may be helpfully constructive or conversely damaging, it is important to establish the actual connection, not the least in the artistic world, because the strong, positive current appreciation and popular affection for 'Impressionism' will have an effect on Degas' reputation; on the other hand, his work will have an influence in creating the popular understanding of the character of the movement.

There is already in this an inherent problem in determining the extent of Degas' association with the movement since there is no doubt that Degas has been so identified by name that his work has inevitably contributed to the perceived content of Impressionism – to this extent his inclusion is something of a self-fulfilling prophesy. To illustrate the point: his studies of ballet dancers are generally perceived as typical of Impressionist painting – which they assuredly are not. Although it is undoubtedly true that the theatre and ballet held great attraction for Degas, both of these pursuits (as with horse racing) are in the purview of the 'gentleman', of the *haute bourgeoisie* and, as such, could be regarded as of proper interest to an élitist class. Manet was the only other figure in the independent group who could have appreciated these subjects, and it is interesting that he was drawn by Degas, at the races.

As has already been noted, the name 'Impressionism' was coined by a critic, Louis Le Roy, to describe the first exhibition of 1874, despite the fact that a number of the exhibitors were not Impressionists. Although Degas was one of the principal organizers, and when one considers the work he exhibited, it is evident that it was of a different order and intention from those who are unquestionably recognizable as Impressionists, especially Monet, Pissarro, Sisley and Renoir.

It is also important to note that Degas never accepted the name for the group and continued to propose that the description Independent was more appropriate, indicating that they did not work in a specific, unified style but were united only in opposition to establishment academicism. Degas eventually persuaded the group that this term should be included in the title. He believed that a Salon for Realists should be created and this gives some indication of his own attitude. He saw his work as presenting those aspects of life that interested or inspired him directly: for him, painting was a way of penetrating reality rather than the creation of an impression.

Some association with Impressionist painting is clear and if exhibiting with and associating with the painters who constituted such a group made Degas one of them, then he is an Impressionist by association. Whether he held any belief in the Impressionist philosophy we shall have to examine further: it is certainly true that Monet's belief in painting on-the-spot to catch the immediate sensation, the fleeting 'impression', was certainly not

PLATE 20
Café-Concert, Les Ambassadeurs (1876-77)
Pastel over monotype, 14^1/$_2$ x 10^2/$_3$ inches (37 x 27cm)

One popular form of entertainment of the Parisian social scene, and frequented by Degas, was the café-concert and one of the most highly regarded was at Les Ambassadeurs, a neo-classical building at the bottom end of the Champs-Elysées. Originally used by the working classes and petits-bourgeois, they had become rather more up-market by the time Degas frequented them. Young men-about-town dined and drank, loudly applauded the singers, and made vulgar comments on their physical charms and it is such a scene that Degas depicts here. Two of the last singers that Degas would have seen performing there were Édith Piaf and Josephine Baker. The technique Degas employed on this occasion was to add pastel heightening to monotype.

PLATE 21
Women in Front of a Café: Evening (Femmes devant un café, le soir: un café sur le Boulevard Montmartre) 1877
Pastel on monotype, 16 x 23^2/$_3$ inches (41 x 60cm)

Degas was fascinated by the café society of Paris and made many studies and paintings of the scene from such poignant works as L'Absinthe (plate 19) to the riotous concert in the previous plate. As usual, they are sketched on-the-spot in crayon and later executed in oil paint, monotype, pastel or essence. Degas was concerned to express the different characters of the young girls, possibly prostitutes, who frequented the open cafés. With Degas' usual individuality, the view is from the inside of the café looking towards the street depicted outside. The central figure has a provocative expression, quite sexy, in contrast to the unattractive dark figure on the right.

PLATE 22
Dancer Taking a Bow (c. 1877) detail
Pastel on paper mounted on canvas,
28¹/₃ x 30¹/₂ inches (72 x 77.5cm)

Of all the subjects used by Degas, his dancers are the ones for which he is best known and are the most widely admired. But it is not necessarily the subject that most engaged his interest. This subject was painted about ten times with or without the bouquet, all at about the same time. When this was painted, the costumes were all appropriate to the action rather than the typically short skirts in which Degas has represented them – a typical example of his disregard for factual realism. As he was often fond of observing, 'one gives the idea of truth with the false'.

Degas' view – he was essentially a studio painter.

Ultimately, and truthfully, one has to say that neither in technique nor intention was Degas ever really an Impressionist painter. The writer and art critic George Moore, who knew Degas at the Nouvelle-Athènes, quoted him as saying: 'No art was less spontaneous than mine. What I do is the result of reflection and study of the great masters; of inspiration, spontaneity, temperament I know nothing.' His search was for an unsentimental reality, a pictorial objectivity essentially of those subjects that interested him such as the racecourse and horses, the theatre and ballet, laundresses at work, and the female form in studies of women bathing. Although he painted landscapes they were not, as with the Impressionists proper, a subject in which he developed his art. In 1892, in a conversation with some friends he said that he had 21 landscapes for exhibition, at which they all protested that he had never done any; but he claimed to have done them all that summer. He said that he had stood at the door of the coach of the train and could see things vaguely. His eyesight by this time was very weak.

Although all the Impressionists were subjected to either vitriolic or dismissive criticism in the early years, by the time of the last exhibition in 1886, the accessibility and attractiveness of Impressionist painting, the evident freshness present in the work, and the recognition of the sterility and irrelevance of the academic approach had

PLATE 23
Ballet Dancer on Stage (c. 1878)
Pastel over monotype on paper, 22¾ x 16½ inches
(58 x 42cm)

*The similarity between this and the previous plate is an example
of Degas' use of the same compositional structures in a number of
different works. The main difference between these two arises from
the squarer shape of the picture area in the former, allowing a
more spacious effect, and the large orange parasols and the*

*grouped figures are associated to provide a secondary interest in the
background. In this second work, the left side of the picture is
similar to the previous one but, because of the higher rectangular
shape, the dancer is depicted near the right edge which provides a
concentrated and more lyrical composition. The dancer is one of
Degas' most elegant portrayals. It is also to be noted that the
dancer is seen from above in a much steeper perspective than in
the previous work which increases the rythmic flow of the painting
by comparison.*

resulted in the public and commercial success of all of the
major figures. The first stage of the Impressionist revolution
had been completed.

For Degas, the period of the Impressionist exhibitions
was a time of mixed emotions. He was gratified to be
recognized as an important 'modern' painter, and was
financially successful; but his eyesight had deteriorated
through the 1880s to the extent that by 1892 he was
effectively obliged to abandon painting in oils. Pastel
remained the only medium open to him; but here his
characteristic precision was appreciably diminished to be
replaced by bold rich colour and simplified drawing. Despite
considerable physical limitations, during this later period he
managed to produce some powerful and commanding work
– almost from memory.

The last important phase in Degas' work began in 1886
when in the final Impressionist exhibition he offered a series
of paintings of women bathing and washing, drying and
combing their hair (plates 35–38). In these works, drawn or
painted largely from memory but with the aid of
photographs, Degas achieves a depth and intensity of
treatment of what he has made seem a private, almost secret,
activity and that makes these late works some of his most
admired. Degas' own comment on these paintings was:
'Hitherto, the nude has always been represented in poses
which presuppose an audience, but these women of mine
are honest, simple folk, unconcerned by any other interests

than those involved in their physical condition.' Here is
another: 'She is washing her feet. It is as if you looked
through the keyhole.' On another occasion he observed,
'See how different times are for us; two hundred years ago I
would have been painting "Susannah bathing", now I just
paint "Woman in a Tub".' George Moore commented:
'... the naked woman has become impossible in modern art;
it required Degas' genius to infuse new life into the worn-
out theme. Cynicism was the greatest means of eloquence
in the Middle Ages, and with cynicism Degas has rendered
the nude again an artistic possibility.' Another general view,
voiced by Degas' friend and pupil, Mary Cassatt, in 1893,
was that he was 'not an easy man to deal with' – an opinion
with which most of his friends would have agreed.

Despite his success, it was not until 1893 that Degas
held his first one-man exhibition – at Paul Durand-Ruel's
new gallery. In 1886, after the last Impressionist exhibition,
Degas had given Durand-Ruel, who was a particular
supporter of the Impressionists, exclusive rights to his work.
Durand-Ruel was one of an increasing number of dealer-
patrons whose collections after the painters' deaths often
became the basis of public collections of the moderns. For
his first exhibition Degas showed, perhaps somewhat
surprisingly since it is not a major element in his *oeuvre*,
mainly landscape pastels and monotypes, which included
those mentioned above.

Degas was most concerned in these later years with his

PLATE 24
Woman with Hats (1905-10)
Pastel on tracing paper, 35⁷/₈ x 29¹/₂ inches (91 x 75cm)

During the early 1880s Degas made a number of paintings and pastels of women at their milliners, trying on hats, chatting and serving customers and these gave him another opportunity to create an atmosphere of intimacy and immediacy. The hats also provided him with the sharp colour points among the more restrained colours of the clothes and interiors. On one visit to a fashionable dressmaker with a friend, Mme. Straus, seeing his concentration, asked what interested him. ' The red hands of the little girl who holds the pins,' was his reply. There is also a feeling of respect and regard in these works. It would have been easy to caricature the posturings of fashionable figures but these works show affection and sympathy. This opens a question never resolved. Degas never married and no love affairs have been substantiated. His sexuality and orientation, as it is now described, is not known. He was a close friend of Mary Cassatt and his favourite models speak well of him. On the other hand, there are reports of sexual impotence, of the effects of venereal disease, including a claim that he had 'a lack of the means of making love'. These beautifully drawn and affectionate studies suggest that he was perhaps not entirely the curmudgeonly misogynist that he is usually described as being.

health – and particularly his eyesight. His preoccupation was such that, although he lived until 1917, and towards the end of the First World War (of which he was only dimly conscious), he was to produce little work and even the larger pastels became problematical. One possibility did, however, remain – modelling in clay. Although he could only dimly discern the forms he produced, they responded to his strong tactility and the sculptures that he produced remain as a potent legacy of the 'inner necessity' of the creative artist. The subjects for his sculpture were drawn from his greatest interests: horses, dancers and women bathing.

In 1898 Degas was reunited with his brother René from whom he had been estranged for many years as a result of René's divorce from his blind wife Estelle. Degas regarded René's behavior as indefensible – a feeling perhaps heightened by his sympathetic recognition of the difficulties her blindness would cause her.

From 1900, Degas became increasingly reclusive. Always a private person, he rarely saw any of his friends who were in any event themselves often incapacitated or had died. He was particularly distressed by the death of his boyhood friend and collector of his work, Henri Rouart, who died in 1912. Rouart's collection of paintings, when

PLATE 25
Miss La La at the Cirque Fernando
(1879) see also page 230
Oil on canvas, 46 x 30¹/₂ inches (117 x 77.5cm)

Mademoiselle La La was a negro or mulatto acrobat, known as la femme canon, who is seen here performing at the most famous of the Paris circuses. Degas, like many of his contemporaries, was intrigued by the circus and the Fernando was very near to his home. He made many preliminary studies for this work, one of his larger oil paintings. It was finished in January 1879 and exhibited in May of that year in the Impressionist exhibition. The striking composition shows La La suspended by her teeth, high up in the elaborate vaulted interior and it is said that Degas had trouble with the perspective of the ceiling and hired a professional to make a drawing for him. This is a unique example in Degas' work of a deliberately realist depiction of a highly dramatic effect and may have been made at La La's request, since he knew her personally.

sold, commanded high prices, *Two Dancers at the Bar with Watering Can* by Degas fetching 475,000 francs – at that time the highest price to be realized by a living artist.

Degas' last years were filled with sadness and he always regretted a move that he was forced to make, in 1912, from his home in the rue Victor Massé, where he had lived for 20 years, to an appartment and studio at 6 boulevard Clichy where, on 27 September 1917, he died. He never married and was buried in the family vault in Montmartre Cemetery. As he observed: ' ...there is love; there is work. And we have but a single heart.' His was devoted to art: 'A painter has no private life.'

In 1914, the great collection of Count Camondo was acquired by the Louvre. It included some of Degas' finest works. With the inclusion of these works in the national collection, the victory of the modern Impressionists over the historicist academics was complete. The early modern movements of the 20th century, Fauvism, Cubism,

PLATE 26
Degas Group Skit (1885)

This group, posed by Degas, is intended as a skit on Ingres' painting, The Apotheosis of Homer, *which had been exhibited to great acclaim in the Salon of 1827. Degas wrote in September 1885 about this photograph. 'It would have been better if I had placed my threes muses (the Lemoisne sisters) and my two choirboys (Elie and Daniel Halévy) in front of a white or light-coloured background. The detail of the ladies' dresses is lost. It would have been better if the figures had been moved more closely together.' Little one feels could have rescued this image from bathos and one is surprised that Degas undertook it. He was 41 at the time!*

PLATE 27
Degas in His Studio (c.1895) opposite

PLATE 28
Portrait of Ludovic Halévy
and Albert Boulanger-Cave (1879)
Pastel and distemper on paper, 31 x 21²/₃ inches
(79 x 55cm)

These two gentlemen, friends of Degas, are depicted at the Opéra where men of repute were permitted to go backstage, thus causing it to develop into a social meeting place. Ludovic Halévy was a special friend of Degas'. Born in the same year, they were close companions until the Dreyfus affair which severed many

friendships and became a cause célèbre prompting Zola's famous pamphlet 'J'Accuse'. Halévy became a librettist (Carmen, La Belle Hélène, La Vie Parisienne) and novelist and is seen in a number of Degas' works. He also illustrated Halévy's story of backstage life with a series of monotypes. Daniel Halévy, Ludovic's son and a great admirer of the painter, is the source of much information on him in the notebooks he kept of Degas' frequent visits during the period of close intimacy Degas maintained with the family. Degas exhibited the painting in the 1879 Impressionist show.

Futurism, and others, were the already recognized avant garde – the new art. After Degas' death, Renoir had a further two years to live, while Monet had nearly ten years of life and active work left to him although nearly all of his other contemporaries died before him.

DEGAS THE ARTIST
In outlining the course of Degas' less than dramatic life, some indication of the qualities and nature of his artistic achievement has been given; but it is necessary to consider his work more fully to understand the special contribution he made, both to his own time and as an inspiration to subsequent painters.

His work changed and matured gradually. The first serious work, recognizably his, is part of the academic historicist tradition while he was still being influenced by his position in society as part of the 'establishment' and hoping for recognition as a successful amateur in a professional world. At that time, artists were accorded intellectual authority, often lionized, and revered by students and members of the intelligentsia. It must be remembered that in the 19th century no art schools existed as we now know them, and most aspiring painters went through a form of apprenticeship with a recognized 'master'. (This was traditional in the Renaissance period when the young Leonardo was apprenticed in the studio of Andrea Verrocchio.) Renoir, Monet, Bazille, Whistler and

PLATE 29
Edmond Duranty (1879)
Gouache and pastel on canvas, 39³/₈ x 39³/₈ inches
(100 x 100cm)

Duranty was a writer and critic and Degas' friend. Degas first met him at the Café Guerbois among Manet's group. He became a strong supporter of Degas and they influenced one another in their work, Duranty naming Degas in one of his novels. His reviews of Degas' works in the Impressionist exhibitions were favourable, as were those of most critics, including Geffroy, Huysmans and Mallarmé. After Duranty died, Degas solicited works from his friends for a sale to raise funds for his widow. This painting is an example of Degas' personal combination of different methods and materials to achieve the end he sought. The books are mainly in gouache (opaque watercolour), while Duranty's head and hands are constructed in pastel. The placing of the figure, and the emphasis on the books which surround him, identify Duranty's profession in a work of great distinction. It has been suggested that it may have influenced Cézanne to also use books in his portrait of Geffroy.

PLATE 30
Hélène Rouart in Her Father's Study (1886)
opposite
Oil on canvas, 64 x 48 inches (162 x 123cm)

Hélène, Henri Rouart's daughter, was born in 1863, the year of the Salon des Refusés, and was a member of a family which Degas held in great affection. This portrait shows her in her 20s as a serious, wistful young lady in a cultured environment, revealing her father's interest in ancient Egyptian art. Degas had first painted Hélène when she was a small child and her red hair attracted him, causing him to write to her father in Venice when she was 20 to say that he would have liked to have joined them in the city 'where her hair and colouring are of the kind so much admired in the past' – recollections of Titian, evidently. As with a number of Degas' works, this painting is uncompleted and he made a number of studies of the composition in a variety of poses and had also at one time intended to include Hélène's mother. Richard Kendall in his catalogue 'Degas: Beyond Impressionism', suggests that work on the painting occurred as late as 1895.

PLATE 31
Diego Martelli (1879) detail above
Oil on canvas, 43¹/₃ x 39³/₈ inches (110 x 100cm)

Diego Martelli was a Neapolitan engraver who worked in Paris and Degas used to drop in for a friendly chat in Italian at his studio where this portrait is located. Degas made fewer portraits as he got older and this is a gesture of friendship. Its informal treatment in the cluttered interior suggests the captured moment rather than the posed figure but, as we observe with his women bathers, it is carefully composed in its informality. The angle of vision is from above, indicating the close proximity of sitter and painter and few painters would balance the figure turned away from a cluttered still-life of table with bric-à-brac. It is typical of Degas, however, as is the bright sharp note of the slippers and the folding chair. The delightful intimacy of the painting makes it one of Degas' uniquely attractive works.

Sisley, for instance, were pupils in Gleyre's Academy. Charles Gleyre was a Swiss painter who took over the studio of Paul Delaroche in Paris where his historical paintings gained him a high reputation at the Salon. Like most painter-teachers, he enjoyed a steady income from his articled charges. He is unusual in that he recognized the qualities of these students and it is perhaps an appropriate footnote to his career that he died in the year of the first Impressionist exhibition in which some of these same pupils exhibited.

Degas' first teacher, as previously mentioned, was Louis Lamothe. He had spent a short period in the studio of a little-known painter, Félix-Joséph Barrias, but Degas' father, Auguste De Gas, is believed to have consulted Valpinçon for advice regarding his son's artistic education who, in turn, is thought to have consulted Ingres who recommended that he should train under one of his own pupils, Louis Lamothe. (De Gas was the family name before the two syllables became joined: the correct pronunciation is therefore with the 'e' unaccented and is not, as is often encountered, pronounced Dégas – Daygas.) Lamothe was a meticulous follower of Ingres although himself a minor figure. The advice was taken and the influence significant. Ingres' well known passion for drawing, and apparent to Degas on their first meeting, was certainly transmitted to him through Lamothe. It became the cornerstone of Degas' art.

PLATE 32
Blue Dancers (c.1890) detail opposite
Oil on canvas, 33⁷/₁₆ x 29³/₄ inches (85 x 75.5cm)

Most of Degas' studies of the ballet were made backstage at the Opéra where he would coax the girls, 'the little rats', to stop a while in order that he could draw them in various poses. These sketches were either worked up further in his studio or formed the basis for a composition containing a number of figures. The sketches were usually in pastel and the groups in pastel, essence or oil although on occasions, particularly in his later work, he used a combinations of all these media.

PLATE 33
Singer in Green (1884) detail below
Pastel on paper, 23 x 18 inches (58.4 x 45.7cms)

A brilliant pastel of a popular entertainer – gaudy, young and precociously confident in a costume of audacious vulgarity and set in a theatrically bright and indeterminate setting. It encapsulates the very nature of popular entertainment in a simple image. Although unknown, the young girl is the quintessential theatrical personality, sensual and engaging in the remote footlights but essentially unreal and probably unattractive in the harsh light of day. The extraordinary quality of Degas' direct draughtsmanship in the immediacy of the pastel technique confirms his mastery of the difficult method.

The essential qualities of drawing are difficult to identify without qualification. For our purposes it might be described as delineating on a surface the intentions of the draughtsman, in materials and in a form that expresses effectively and accurately his intention. In a charming and now well known explanation, a small child described drawing thus: 'I think and then I draw a line around my think.' Perhaps this is a better way of expressing the nature of drawing than any more elaborate definition, including the one above. Ingres was regarded as the great academic draughtsman of the age and Lamothe's stressing of the importance of drawing struck a positive chord in Degas, although he had little regard for Lamothe himself. Drawing became the backbone of Degas' art from this early stage. The ability does not, however, come God-given and fully formed. It must be worked upon, and for Degas this meant a constant devotion to drawing a great variety of subjects in many different media. From early academic studies and through the course of his life, as with all great draughtsmen, he developed a freer, more adaptable and adventurous method and his later drawings, less precise and bolder, though sensitive and penetrating, represent some of the finest examples of draughtsmanship that we have.

It must always be remembered, however, that drawing is not solely or even mainly a linear activity. The definition offered in the previous paragraph does not specify thin pencil or pen-drawn line and drawing with a brush, chalk,

PLATE 34
Women Ironing (c. 1884-86) detail
Oil on canvas, 30 x 32 inches (76 x 81.5cm)

A subject that attracted Degas but resulted in relatively few paintings, this was possibly inspired by the Goncourt brothers whose writing Degas admired. Apart from their famous Journal, a chatty and imaginative gossip about Parisian life, they wrote novels and in the introduction to one of them observed: 'We have asked ourselves if what one calls the "lower classes" have not a right to a novel.' Degas' interest may have been thus stimulated by the sight of the many laundresses who were constantly to be seen on the streets with their parcels of laundry for the gentry. For the earliest depiction in 1869 of a girl ironing, Degas used a model and later produced from sketches a number of studies of laundresses, including the late one illustrated. Here the squalid, barren scene reveals the two figures in a carefully balanced composition with Degas' special use of colour very evident; the orange, red and pink notes enliven the scene composed of blues, greens and greys. The careful delineation of the tired or drunken figure on the left is balancing the less distinct figure concentrating on her work, on the right. Is there a psychological message in the different treatments, or is it reality?

pastel and even a spatula or fingers is not excluded. Drawing is a part of painting and, indeed, sculpture. It is the expression of the defined sensitivity of the artist in any medium.

One of Degas' favourite methods was pastel-painting. There are certain specific qualities in pastel that are attractive to the artist. The ideal for any painter is that his intention should be immediately achieved and evident and that it should not change with time. There are many reasons why changes should occur in painting, both physical and chemical, and the method least subject to such changes is pastel which is applied to the surface as almost pure colour with few additives to affect it. This leaves the surface in a delicate condition but the colour is the purest expression of the artist's intention that can be achieved. It was this immediacy of effect that attracted Degas, especially in subjects where movement was inherent such as in horses or dancers. It might be noted that it is possible to use a fixative for pastel that has a minimal effect on it, helping it to retain its brilliance longer than either watercolour or oil. This may partly account for the popularity of Degas' pastels whose brilliance is apparent to all observers. Although there are a number of earlier, particularly 18th-century, pastellists of considerable ability, they operated mainly as portraitists (less expensive and more direct than oil portraits) and Degas explored the use of pastel in a range of

PLATE 35

Woman Brushing Her Hair (c. 1885) detail

Pastel on card, $20^7/_8$ x $20^1/_2$ inches (53 x 52cm)

In his late works depicting women engaged in bathing and associated activities, which continued from the 1870s to the end of his active career, Degas frequently chose the subject of women combing their hair or having it combed by a maid. The paintings appear to be casual, unobserved studies of the nude but are constructed from studies of models or directly from models in the studio. What Degas himself described as a 'keyhole' effect is in fact a studied artificial realism which produces a convincing voyeuristic result and there has been much discussion on the importance of these works and their revolutionary character. Degas, as noted on page 272, made the point that had his nudes been painted earlier they would have been given a literary, biblical or historical title, such as 'Susannah bathing', but that now he would call them merely The Tub *(plate 36). This pastel is an exquisitely drawn study of a woman's back in the subtlest colour and is the result of many sketches.*

effects and with such marked sensitivity that he may be regarded as one of greatest practitioners of the method. His contemporary, Odilon Redon, was also a fine pastellist but his work was part of the Symbolist mysticism and his colour has an expressionist intensity in sharp contrast to Degas' sensitive realism; together they reveal the range possible in this responsive medium.

Degas also employed two further techniques, usually or often in conjunction with pastel. These are not commonly used but Degas found them useful, particularly as his sight deteriorated and made precision difficult for him. They are the use of monotype and painting with essence rather than oil. Monotype is a method of transferring an image painted on glass onto paper, pressed onto the glass and pulled free so that most of the paint, in no way absorbed into the glass, leaves a less than complete image on the paper which may then by drawn on with pastel. More than one print can be produced from a single subject in this way, making alternative colour sketches possible. Essence painting consists in using an essential oil such as oil of cloves, or lavender or spikenard. This gives something of the effect of thin watercolour but with more opacity in the colour, providing a more 'solid' effect. Degas applied pastel to both monotype and essence sketches.

Degas was nevertheless a trained practitioner in oil painting and here, too, he developed a mastery of the method adopted by the majority of professional painters.

The versatility of oils as a method has been noted by most observers. From the finest and most detailed, to the broadest and most free applications of paint, the oil method responds exceptionally well. The type and form of the brushes or other applicators determines the quality and character of the work more than the method itself. In this century we have become accustomed to paint being applied with great freedom and some disregard for permanence, but in the 19th century and earlier, the attitude to the creation of a work of art was that it should be important enough to be revered and preserved. Experiment was dangerous, the most famous example of this being Leonardo's attempt to use oil on a plaster wall for the *Last Supper* in Milan – its ruinous state a witness to the failure. This necessitated a concern for the method itself, the use of the finest materials and the longest lasting pigments, as well as knowledge of their chemical interaction. There were well known exceptions to this. For instance, J. M.W. Turner, in his pursuit of effect, was capable of achieving results which would inevitably ensure the quick deterioration of the work. But most painters, Degas included, were careful technicians.

The preparation of the canvas or board was significant to the final effect, and canvases were usually prepared with a white ground. Historically, canvases and colours were prepared in the studios by the assistants, but during the 19th century manufacturers and colour shops appeared and

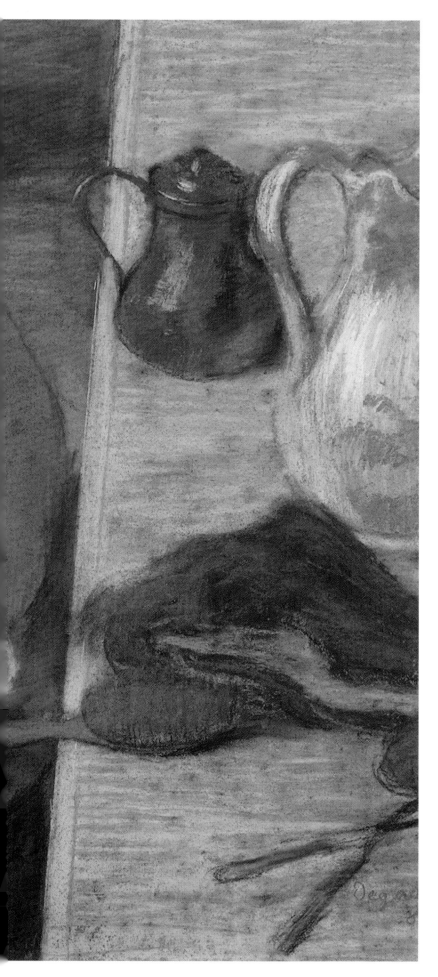

PLATE 36
The Tub (1886) detail
Pastel on card, 23²/₃ x 32²/₃ inches (60 x 83cm)

*This famous work shows many aspects of Degas' methods.
Firstly, it will be noted that the sense of intimacy that he has
achieved is the result of the steep perspective of the table-top
which, when analysed, is clearly seen to be inaccurate in relation
to the objects on it, which are viewed (to make their supporting
role as a curved shape behind the figure visually convincing) from
a lower eye-level. At the same time the figure is seen from
immediately above and the viewer looks almost directly down into
the circular tub. More might be said on this compositional matter
but it is another occasion on which Degas uses visual devices to
convey a sense of the truth. The draughtsmanship is as acute as
always and it is apparent that despite the deterioration of his
eyesight, he is still able to produce a closely modelled image and
subtle colour relationships in this sympathetic and tender work.
Huysman's comments on this pastel are somewhat different. He
describes the figure as 'a red-haired corpulent swollen female' but
goes on to say that 'never have works been so lacking in slyness
or questionable overtones'. The pastel was shown with others in
the series in the eighth and last Impressionist exhibition of 1886.*

PLATE 37
After the Bath, Woman Drying Her Feet
(1886)

Pastel on paper, 21³/₈ x 20⁵/₈ inches (54.3 x 52.4cm)

With all the studies of women engaged in their toilette there are usually a number of versions, some almost identical, some with variations. This is one of the more completely resolved works of great authority. It is interesting to note the vertical dark area on the right suggestive, perhaps, of an open door and implying the sense of security of the bather but a voyeurist artist peering in. It was exhibited in the Impressionist show of 1886.

PLATE 38
After the Bath (c.1885) pages 70–71
Pastel, 18⁷/₈ x 34¹/₄ inches (48 x 87cm)

This seems to have been an attractive pose for Degas' studies since it appears, although in reverse, in his early academic painting Scene of War in the Middle Ages *(plate 5), almost exactly similarly placed.*

the painters in Degas' day usually patronized them. In general, painters were supplied with what they needed but, as is the unfortunate way of commerce, adulteration in order to save money and thereby make more profit began to increasingly occur and the artists most concerned with their own work often continued to grind and mix their own pigments. During the 1840s, pigment colours in tubes became available and this had a liberating effect on painters in two major respects: firstly, it obviated the lengthy preparation of the traditional method and secondly, it enabled artists to paint out-of-doors where and when they wished without having to carry heavy materials about with them. This last was a great advantage to Impressionists like Monet but of no great interest to Degas who, as we have noted, deplored *plein-air* painting. In this century, the tubed paints, often manufactured from coal-tar dyes, have come to dominate the market.

The problems caused by Degas' deteriorating vision during and after the 1870s meant that consideration of technique became secondary to him, his main concern being to produce an image that was visually acceptable. With pastels, this meant a larger than usual picture area and more brilliant colour as his perception of colour weakened. The result with pastels, as also with oils, was to increase the intensity of colour and tonal variation and to lessen the precision, so important to him, of his drawing.

Continued on page 296

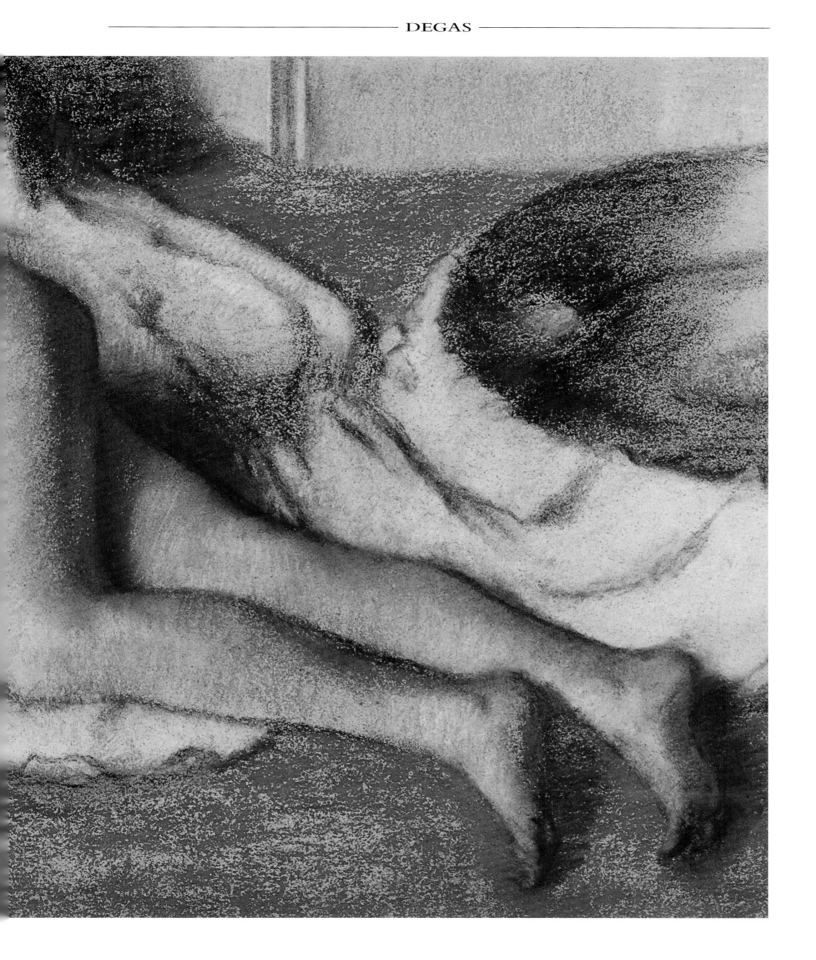

PLATE 39
The Little Dancer Aged Fourteen (1878–81)
opposite
Bronze with muslin skirt and satin hair ribbon, on
wooden base. Height excluding base 39 inches (99cm)

PLATE 40
Dancer Fastening the Strings of Her Tights
(1895-90) top right
Bronze. Height 16¹⁄₂ inches (42cm)

PLATE 41
**Arabesque over the Right Leg, Left Arm in
Front** (1892-95) below right
Bronze. Height 8 inches (20cm)

*The subject of Degas' sculpture has been, for the most of the
period since his death, given a minor place in the consideration of
his oeuvre and it is only recently that a reassessment of its
content and importance has been made. Curated by Richard
Kendall, exhibitions at the National Gallery, London and the
Art Institute of Chicago have drawn attention to its significance,
through his introductory essays. Most of the sculptures have been
translated into bronze in very limited editions which have
allowed both a greater familiarity and serious misapprehension.
According to Vollard, Degas '...could not take the responsibility
of leaving anything behind him in bronze; that metal, he felt
was for eternity.' His sculptures were all created in either 'red
wax' or in clay and cast in plaster. And although the Little
Dancer Aged Fourteen is a well known work and now in
bronze, it is only one of a number created in wax and added
materials, such as ribbons and tulle. They were also well known
by his contemporaries although Degas did not exhibit them.
George Moore, a keen observer of the art of the period, saw them
and commented: '...dancing girls modelled in red wax, some
dressed in muslin skirts, strange dolls – dolls if you wish, but
dolls modelled by a man of genius'. Others, including Renoir,
who saw these works in Degas' studio thought they were of great
significance. Richard Kendall says that Louisine Havemeyer,
Mary Cassatt's great friend, tried unsuccessfully in 1903 to buy
the Little Dancer and considered it 'one of the greatest works of
art since the dynasties of the Nile'. It was intended to be shown
in the 1880 Impressionist show, but was not finished and was
included in the show the following year. The bronze version in
an unknown number was made starting in 1922.*

PLATE 42
Horse With Lowered Head (c.1895–90)
Bronze. Height 7 inches (18cm)

Degas' interest in horses started early and his painting and pastels of racecourse subjects signalled his abandonment of academic restraints. The vitality and knowledge to be found in his sculptured horses indicates this continued passion into later life.

Continued from page 291

As has already been mentioned, one activity was a great help as Degas' sight-loss increasingly prevented him from seeing the images that he was creating. His acute sense of touch enabled him to model forms in clay. These were usually small figures of dancers, of women bathing or drying themselves after bathing, of horses in various stages of motion. These tactile creations were an *aide mémoire* to the pastels, monotypes and essence paintings, often with pastel additions. These sculptures together form another important element of the total Degas *oeuvre*.

The few specific examples here will illuminate the development of the variety and quality of his use of the different techniques outlined above and illustrated in this book.

The summation of Degas' achievement was to add a distinctive technique and traditional qualities to the output of the revolutionary movement which is known as Impressionism. The extension of the Impressionist contribution is present in the painters known as Post-Impressionists, although they were the contemporaries of Degas. The four most important of these were Cézanne, Seurat, Gauguin and Van Gogh – all of whom died over a decade before Degas himself died.

The Publishers wish to thank the following for providing photographs, and for permission to reproduce copyright material. While every effort has been made to trace and acknowledge copyright-holders, we wish to apologize should any omissions have been made.

Self-Portrait with Crayon

Musée d'Orsay/Giraudon, Paris

René-Hilaire De Gas

Musée d'Orsay/Giraudon, Paris

The Bellelli Family

Musée d'Orsay/Giraudon, Paris

Semiramis Founding Babylon

Musée d'Orsay/Giraudon, Paris

Scene of War in the Middle Ages

Musée d'Orsay/Giraudon, Paris

Self-Portrait with Hat

Calouste Gulbenkian Museum, Lisbon/Giraudon, Paris

Gentleman's Race: Before the Start

Musée d'Orsay/Giraudon, Paris

At the Racecourse, With Jockeys in Front of the Stands

Musée d'Orsay/Giraudon, Paris

Amateur Jockeys on the Course, beside an Open Carriage

Musée d'Orsay/Lauros/Giraudon, Paris

Léon Bonnat

Musée Bonnat, Bayonne/Giraudon, Paris

Thérèse De Gas

Musée d'Orsay/Lauros/Giraudon, Paris

Interior Scene, known as The Rape

Philadelphia Museum of Art,
Collection Henry Macilhenny/Bridgeman/Giraudon, Paris

The Orchestra of the Opéra, Rue Le Peletier

Musée d'Orsay/Giraudon, Paris

Jeantaud, Linet and Lainé

Musée d'Orsay/Giraudon, Paris

The Cotton Exchange at New Orleans

Musée des Beaux-Arts, Pau/Giraudon, Paris

The Pedicure

Musée d'Orsay/Lauros/Giraudon, Paris

The Dancing Class

Musée d'Orsay/Lauros/Giraudon, Paris

Dancers Resting

Christie's, London/Bridgeman/Giraudon, Paris

L'Absinthe

Musée d'Orsay/Bridgeman/Giraudon, Paris

Café-Concert, Les Ambassadeurs

Musée des Beaux-Arts, Lyon/Giraudon, Paris

Women in Front of a Café: Evening (Femmes devant un café, le soir: un café sur le Boulevard Montmartre)

Louvre/Giraudon, Paris

Dancer Taking a Bow

Musée d'Orsay/Giraudon, Paris

Ballet Dancer on Stage

Musée d'Orsay/Lauros/Giraudon, Paris

Woman with Hats

Musée d'Orsay/Giraudon, Paris

Miss La La at the Cirque Fernando

The National Gallery, London/Bridgeman/Giraudon, Paris

Degas Group Skit

Hulton Getty

Degas in His Studio

Hulton Getty

Portrait of Ludovic Halévy and Albert Boulanger-Cave

Glasgow Art Gallery, Scotland/Bridgeman/Giraudon, Paris

Edmond Duranty

Glasgow Art Gallery, Scotland/Bridgeman/Giraudon, Paris

Hélène Rouart in Her Father's Study

The National Gallery, London/Giraudon, Paris

Diego Martelli

National Gallery of Scotland, Edinburgh

Blue Dancers

Musée d'Orsay/Giraudon, Paris

Singer in Green

Trewin Copplestone

Women Ironing

Musée d'Orsay/Giraudon, Paris

Woman Brushing Her Hair

Hermitage Museum, St. Petersburg/Giraudon, Paris

The Tub

Musée d'Orsay/Lauros/Giraudon, Paris

After the Bath, Woman Drying Her Feet

Toronto Art Gallery, Canada/Giraudon, Paris

After the Bath

Musée du Louvre, Cabinet des Dessins, Paris

The Little Dancer Aged Fourteen

Christie's, London, Private Collection/Bridgeman Art Library, London

Dancer Fastening the Strings of Her Tights

San Diego Museum of Art/Bridgeman Art Library

Arabesque Over the Right Leg, Left Arm in Front

Fitzwilliam Museum, University of Cambridge/Bridgeman Art Library,

Horse With Lowered Head

Fitzwilliam Museum, University of Cambridge/Bridgeman Art Library